The
STRENGTH
YOU NEED

THE TWELVE GREAT STRENGTH
PASSAGES OF THE BIBLE

ROBERT J. MORGAN

W PUBLISHING GROUP

AN IMPRINT OF THOMAS NELSON

Published in Nashville, Tennessee, by W Publishing Group, an imprint of Thomas Nelson. W Publishing and Thomas Nelson are registered trademarks of HarperCollins Christian Publishing, Inc.

Published in association with Yates & Yates, www.yates2.com.

Thomas Nelson titles may be purchased in bulk for educational, business, fund-raising, or sales promotional use. For information, please e-mail SpecialMarkets@ThomasNelson.com.

Unless otherwise noted, Scripture quotations are taken from the Holy Bible, New International Version®, NIV®. © 1973, 1978, 1984, 2011 by Biblica, Inc.® Used by permission of Zondervan. All rights reserved worldwide.

Scripture quotations marked ESV are taken from the ESV® Bible (The Holy Bible, English Standard Version®). © 2001 by Crossway, a publishing ministry of Good News Publishers. Used by permission. All rights reserved. Scripture quotations marked KJV are taken from the Holy Bible, King James Version (public domain). Scripture quotations marked THE MESSAGE are taken from *The Message* by Eugene H. Peterson. © 1993, 1994, 1995, 1996, 2000, 2001, 2002. Used by permission of Tyndale House Publishers, Inc. Scripture quotations marked NKJV are taken from the New King James Version®. © 1982 by Thomas Nelson. Used by permission. All rights reserved. Scripture quotations marked PHILLIPS are taken from J. B. Phillips: The New Testament in Modern English, Revised Edition. © J. B. Phillips 1958, 1960, 1972. Used by permission of Macmillan Publishing Co., Inc. Scripture quotations marked THE VOICE are taken from The Voice™. © 2012 by Ecclesia Bible Society. Used by permission. All rights reserved. Scripture quotations marked TLB are taken from The Living Bible. © 1971. Used by permission of Tyndale House Publishers, Inc., Carol Stream, Illinois 60188. All rights reserved.

ISBN 978-0-7852-1636-0 (TP)
ISBN 978-0-7180-8151-5 (eBook)

Library of Congress Cataloging-in-Publication Data is on
file with the publisher and the Library of Congress.

ISBN 978-0-7180-7959-8 (HC)

17 18 19 20 21 LSC 6 5 4 3 2 1

The
STRENGTH
YOU NEED

OTHER BOOKS BY ROBERT J. MORGAN

To Liam

Contents

CONTENTS

The Sovereign LORD is my *strength*; he makes my feet like the feet
of a deer, he enables me to tread on the heights. Habakkuk 3:19

Love the Lord your God with all your . . . *strength*. Mark 12:30

[Abraham] did not waver through unbelief regarding
the promise of God, but was *strengthened* in his
faith and gave glory to God. Romans 4:20

I pray that out of his glorious riches he may *strengthen* you with
power through his Spirit in your inner being. Ephesians 3:16

I can do all this through him who gives me *strength*. Philippians 4:13

Extra Strength for Every Day

Worn out?

If you're tired today, you need more than rest; you need replenishment and rejuvenation. You need an infusion of power in the hidden core of your personality. My wife, Katrina, and I call this: *Extra Strength*.

Katrina has battled multiple sclerosis for more than a quarter-century, and for the last several years she's been confined to a wheelchair. During this time, I've tried to maintain a regular and busy schedule, adding "caregiver" to my roles and obligations and trying, usually successfully, to do it with a positive spirit. Because of our faith, we're both highly motivated, and neither of us likes to slow down or give up. But recently I've felt a little tired, and so has Katrina. The other day as we sat on the porch of our home in Roan Mountain, Tennessee, Katrina said, "Robert, will you bring me that bottle of extra strength pills from the kitchen?"

"Why?" I asked. "Do you have a headache?"

"No," she said. "It's the *extra strength* I need."

At first I thought she was kidding, but she wasn't; so I retrieved the bottle and studied it. Sure enough, there on the label was a blood-red designation: *Extra Strength*. I gave her a couple of pills—and even took two for myself. We chuckled at the experience, but it represents so much of what we all look for in our desire to find more inner power.

That little episode set me thinking: Where can we really find the extra strength required for each day? How do we build ourselves up when we've worn ourselves out?

I'm sure you know what it's like to be tired. Perhaps you feel exhausted right now. When our strength ebbs, it affects our emotions, which affects our relationships. The Devil knows our frailties, and he knows when we're bleak and weak. Our bodies, minds, and souls are wondrously intertwined, so when we droop in one area, it has a cascading effect. The Bible says, "If you falter in a time of trouble, how small is your strength!" (Prov. 24:10).

Yet we *do* falter and we *do* need extra strength.

That means getting exercise, rest, and good nutrition and staying as healthy as we can. But there's more. Our physical strength is enhanced by our mental attitudes or, conversely, impaired by them; and our mental attitudes are empowered or polluted by the wellsprings of the heart. That day on the porch, Katrina and I weren't on the verge of collapse, but we did feel the weariness that periodically seeps into our bones whatever our age or stage in life. Katrina often needs strength for the simplest tasks, and I need strength for everything from homemaking to globetrotting.

So do you. After all, we're living in a difficult age, and events on the world stage are disconcerting. In times like these, we need to be stronger husbands, stronger wives, and stronger people. We need stronger children, stronger families, stronger churches, and a stronger determination to tackle each day for good and for God. If you're like me, you want stronger faith, stronger peace, stronger joy, and more stamina to do the work the Lord assigns each day.

I long for the inner resources to stay afloat during crises and to rally the spirits of others. I want to be more tenacious, to persevere, to be undiscouraged, and undeterred. I want to be fortified against temptation and intimidation. I want to press through today into tomorrow with all the toughness I can find, doing all this through Christ who strengthens me. And I want to do it all with optimism and joy.

That requires enormous strength, which is not only a universal need but also a moral obligation. We *ought* to be strong. We're *told* to be strong. The Bible commands us: "Be strong in the Lord and in his mighty power" (Eph. 6:10). That's a frequent call in Scripture. The command "Be strong" occurs about forty times in the Bible from Deuteronomy 31:6 ("Be strong and courageous. Do not be afraid or terrified . . . for the LORD your God goes with you; he will never leave you nor forsake you") to 2 Timothy 2:1 ("You then, my son, be strong in the grace that is in Christ Jesus").

It's funny that Katrina's request for extra strength pills triggered all these thoughts in my mind, but that's how it happened. The next morning I decided to look up the word "strength" in the Bible. I did it in the simplest way. I didn't analyze any Hebrew or Greek words. Didn't use a variety of translations. Didn't open a lexicon or any linguistic aids. Didn't conduct an academic study of the word or even look up parallel terms like *strong, might,* or *power.* That would have been too much. There are so many verses and passages on these topics I would have been overwhelmed with references.

Even my initial scanning of the topic was daunting. The subject of extra strength pervades the Bible, which is what we'd expect from an almighty God. The Bible hums with the energy of divine omnipotence, and every page is powerful. The gospel is the power of God unto salvation, and the Word of God itself is alive and powerful, sharper than a two-edged sword.

Everywhere we turn in Scripture, we see references to strength, might, power, energy, and omnipotence. The God of Scripture never grows weak or weary, and no amount of exertion can diminish His energy or resolve. He is majestic in power, and nothing is too hard for Him. His authority keeps the universe percolating without the slightest interruption or abeyance, for, as we read in Romans 1:20, "Since the creation of the world God's invisible qualities—his eternal power and divine nature—have been clearly seen, being understood from what has been made." Hebrews 1:3 says that

Jesus Christ, who "is the radiance of God's glory and the exact representation of His being, sustain[s] all things by His powerful word."

The Bible repeatedly says, "God is able . . ." (Dan. 4:37; Rom. 14:4; 16:25; 2 Cor. 9:8; Eph. 3:20; 2 Tim. 1:12; Heb. 2:18; 5:2; 7:25; Rev. 5:5). Jeremiah said, "No one is like you, LORD; you are great, and your name is mighty in power" (Jer. 10:6). All things are possible for Him who can do all things (Matt. 19:26).

This isn't just a theoretical subject. According to Ephesians 1:19–20, His incomparably great power is available "for us who believe. That power is the same as the mighty strength he exerted when he raised Christ from the dead."

The heroes of the Bible knew how to tap into this dynamic. The apostle Peter said, "His divine power has given us everything we need" (2 Peter 1:3). The apostle Paul spoke of "all the energy Christ so powerfully works in me" (Col. 1:29). To the prophet Isaiah, the Lord said:

> So do not fear, for I am with you;
> Do not be dismayed, for I am your God.
> I will strengthen you and help you;
> I will uphold you with my righteous right hand. (Isa. 41:10)

I didn't have the strength to look up all the synonyms of *strength* in the Bible, so I contented myself to look up the words *strength* and *strengthened* as they occur in just one translation. Even at that, I found more than two hundred references. Thumbing through each of them, I isolated several passages that spoke to my exact need. I adopted them as my *extra strength* verses. Katrina and I have worked on memorizing them. We've meditated on them as we arise in the morning and retire in the evening. As we study them, we feel like we're connecting our 40-watt lives to the nuclear reactor of the very personality of God.

Katrina and I bear these promises in mind when weakened by stress and strain. We've found few subjects more relevant. Our world today is enamored with strength: core strength, upper body strength, lower body strength, military strength, industrial strength, financial strength, emotional strength, personal strength, peace through strength, strength through peace. On the other hand, society views weakness as a liability. Who wants to hike through a dark forest with a weak flashlight, for example, or look for a job in a weak economy? Yet strength and weakness come and go, ebbing and flowing like tides backwashing into the harbors of our own hearts. Sometimes we feel weak as water, and we need extra strength. But the secret to extra strength isn't so much found in *medication* as in *meditation*. It's not extra strength *pills* we need, but extra strength *passages* from God's Word.

From my investigation of this term in Scripture, I chose twelve passages, studied them in depth, sought to claim them for myself, and taught them in a series of presentations under the title "Riveting Strength," and that's the background for this book.

In the following pages we'll set up our drills and derricks so we can tap into the Bible's strength passages like oilmen in the Coyote Hills. The only way to siphon out the needed deposits of personal strength is by drilling deeply into our relationship with the One whom Ambrose of Milan called the "God of all the strength and power."[1] That requires boring through the strata of Scripture—but there's nothing boring about that. Along the way, you'll meet some fascinating people who've discovered for themselves how to tap into God's extra strength and build themselves up when they've worn themselves out.

Here, then, are the dozen verses Katrina and I want to share with you as, according to Psalm 84, we set our hearts on pilgrimage, going from strength to strength till each of us appears before God in Zion. These are our strength strategies from Scripture.

In the following chapters, I want to show you these Gibraltar verses, explain their context, and give examples of how to apply them to life today. Katrina will occasionally chime in too. Keep an open Bible beside you as you read, underline the verses that most speak to you, pass along the salient points to others, and join Katrina and me as we find strength for the weary.

You can be stronger than you are. May the Lord use these twelve biblical passages and promises—and others as you find them in God's Word—to give you "strength for today and bright hope for tomorrow."[2]

ONE

Connect to a High Voltage Line

Your strength will equal your days.

DEUTERONOMY 33:25

In the list of American presidents, one man shows up twice—Grover Cleveland, the only chief executive to serve two non-consecutive terms. He occupies the twenty-second and twenty-fourth spots in the roll call of presidents. He's also the man who dedicated the Statue of Liberty in New York Harbor, and he's the only president to have gotten married in the White House. He was forty-nine at the time; his bride, Frances Folsom, was twenty-one, making her the youngest First Lady in history. Their romance took the nation by storm.

Grover Cleveland was a Presbyterian preacher's kid who was thoroughly trained in Christian truth. He grappled with titanic issues in office, and in the middle of a national financial panic, he faced a personal crisis. He was diagnosed with cancer and endured top-secret surgery aboard a friend's yacht, the news of which was hidden from the nation for years. Nevertheless Cleveland kept up his strength and routinely worked past midnight. Historians have lauded him for his industry, integrity, courage, and common sense. His dying words summed up his life: "I have tried so hard to do right."

The secret of President Cleveland's energy is found in the motto he lived by. It was a biblical promise, which he framed and hung directly over his bed so he could see it every night on retiring and every morning when awakening. I don't know who crafted the engraving for him, but he valued it so highly that it hung on the wall of his law office before his election and afterward in his bedroom at the White House. Throughout his life, he kept it within eyesight. It contained a family crest, beneath which were a set of words taken from the King James Version of Deuteronomy 33:25:

As thy days, so shall thy strength be.

When asked about it, Cleveland said, "If I have any coat of arms and emblem, it is that."[1] He awoke every morning with the firm conviction God would give him the strength required for the work assigned. He believed God would give him sufficient strength for each day's tasks as long as he lived.

That promise can sustain all of us when we awaken in the morning and when we retire at night. It's a lifelong promise of lifetime strength. The Living Bible puts it: "May your strength match the length of your days!" The Amplified Bible renders it: "As your day are, so will your strength, your rest and security be." As I've studied it in the New International Version, I've relished the simple words "Your strength will equal your days."

That's a line in the Bible with high voltage. This biblical promise is so relevant to our lives the writer of the hymn "How Firm a Foundation" devoted an entire stanza to it, saying:

In every condition, in sickness, in health;
In poverty's vale, or abounding in wealth;

At home and abroad, on the land, on the sea,
As thy days may demand, shall thy strength ever be.[2]

In its immediate context in Deuteronomy 33, this verse was originally spoken to the descendants of a man named Asher. Perhaps you've never studied this biblical character, for he's not as well-known as Peter, Paul, David, or Abraham. But as I traced his story through the Bible, I found four great passages that brought him and his descendants to life and helped me better appreciate the promise God gave them in Deuteronomy 33:25.

ASHER'S BIRTH IN GENESIS 30

The story of Asher's birth is told in Genesis 30, where we learn the Patriarch Jacob had twelve sons by four different women. These boys were the great-grandsons of Abraham and the grandsons of Isaac, and they became the founders of the twelve tribes of Israel. Asher was number eight. He was the second son of his mother, Zilpah, but the eighth son of his father, Jacob. Asher's birth announcement is given in Genesis 30:12–13:

> Leah's servant Zilpah bore Jacob a second son. Then Leah said, "How happy I am! The women will call me happy." So she named him Asher.

Asher is a Hebrew word meaning "happy," and this is the first time the word "happy" occurs in the Bible. Think of it! This boy was named Happy, not because he was happy himself—though I suspect he was probably a happy person by temperament—but because, from the beginning of his life, he made others happy. That's a great name to bear. We should all be named that—Happy or Blessed or One Who Makes Others Happy.

Despite his convivial name, the Bible devotes little ink to Asher as he grew up. We don't know much about him, and the book of Genesis reveals little of his actions or activities. In classical Jewish rabbinical literature, he's described as a wise man who did his best to maintain harmony among his quarreling brothers. He was thought to be a reconciler, a peacemaker. Those are only the traditions about him, but somehow I think they're accurate.

ASHER'S BLESSING IN GENESIS 49

The next time we see Asher is near the end of Genesis, in chapter 49, as he and his siblings gathered at the deathbed of their father, Jacob. The old Patriarch rallied his strength to give each son a final blessing. We can visualize the scene as Jacob propped himself on pillows, leaned forward, looked around the room, and addressed every son in turn, giving prophecies to each one. When he came to Asher, he had a short but special prediction, which is recorded in Genesis 49:20: "Asher's food will be rich; he will provide delicacies fit for a king."

In other words, Jacob, who perhaps realized his son had a green thumb, was pronouncing a blessing or a prediction that the descendants of Asher would be food producers, and their products would be the best in Israel. The implication: they would be a happy tribe, living up to their name and making others happy with the richest and finest of food and drink.

ASHER'S TRIBE IN DEUTERONOMY 33

After Jacob died, his descendants multiplied to become a great nation and were enslaved in Egypt until Moses came and delivered them in the exodus and led them into the wilderness toward the promised land. While wandering around in the desert, Moses conducted a census. There were 41,500 young men of the tribe of Asher strong enough to bear arms in the developing Israelite army (Num. 1:41). Asher wasn't the largest or the smallest of the twelve tribes; it was mid-sized. A generation later another census occurred and the number had grown to 53,400 (Num. 26:47).

When the time came to possess the promised land, Moses handed the reins of leadership to Joshua. In Deuteronomy 33, the aged lawgiver gathered the tribes of Israel around him and pronounced a blessing on each one, just as Jacob had earlier done to their forefathers. These blessings comprised Moses' last recorded words.

Deuteronomy 33 is a sort of reenactment of Genesis 49. Just as Jacob, when dying, blessed each of his twelve sons, so Moses, just before vanishing from the scene, blessed each of the twelve tribes that descended from those sons.

From tribe to tribe, from blessing to blessing, we follow the heart of Moses in Deuteronomy 33 as he prayed for each one. In verse 24, he pronounced his blessing on the Happy Tribe, the Asherites, whom Moses described as "most blessed," that is, "most happy."

About Asher he said: "Most blessed of sons is Asher; let him be favored by his brothers, and let him bathe his feet in oil."

Interestingly, some people believe this was a secret prophecy regarding petroleum deposits in the Asherite territory of Israel. In recent years, one oil company began drilling for oil in this area, influenced by this verse.[3] While I hope petroleum discoveries are found in Israel, I don't think that's the intent of Deuteronomy 33:24. This is talking about olive oil, not fossil fuel; and it harkens back to Jacob's prayer for the agricultural success of the tribe of Asher. Abraham and Moses were praying that olive groves and grape vineyards would blanket the hills of Asher. It was a prayer for the rich production of olive oil in such abundance people could bathe their feet in it.

That's exactly what happened. Shortly afterward, when the promised land was divided up and allocated among the twelve tribes, Asher received a prized strip of land in the northern regions of Israel bordering the Mediterranean Sea (Josh. 19:24–31). If overlaid on a modern map, it would run from the Israeli city of Haifa northward all the way to the city of Tyre in southern Lebanon. This is some of the richest agricultural sod in the Middle East with a mild climate and abundant rainfall. It was a breadbasket in biblical times and was especially known for its olive orchards. In times of abundance and drought, Asher provided olive oil and agricultural products for the nation of Israel.

But Moses wasn't done. In Deuteronomy 33:25, he prayed for the territory of Asher to be fortified and protected: "The bolts of your gates will be iron and bronze." These were the strongest metals known in that day, and it was symbolic of homeland security.

Then comes our key verse—the wonderful last half of Deuteronomy 33:25:

. . . and your strength will equal your days.

Moses, then, promised the tribe of Asher an agriculturally fruitful territory with an abundance of olive orchards, with well-fortified cities, and with perpetual strength. He prayed that as long as the tribe of Asher existed, it would possess strength—strength equal to its days. As long as you're alive, Moses told them, you will have the strength you need to do what God assigns and you will have strength to bear whatever each day brings.

But there's more. Verses 26–27 go on to say: "There is no one like the God of Jeshurun [the God of the Upright], who rides across the heavens to help you and on the clouds in his majesty. The eternal God is your refuge, and underneath are the everlasting arms."[4]

With those words Moses wrapped up his final message to Israel, gazed a final time across the multitudes, and then climbed Mount Nebo, where he passed away and was buried in an unmarked grave (Deut. 34:6). The blessings in Deuteronomy 33, then, represent the final words of Moses.

ASHER'S DESCENDANT IN LUKE 2

There's an addendum to the story—something that happened fourteen centuries later in the New Testament. At the dawn of the gospel age, when Jesus was born in Bethlehem in Luke 2, Joseph and Mary took their newborn to the temple in nearby Jerusalem for His dedication. There they encountered an elderly woman named Anna.

> There was also a prophet, Anna, the daughter of Penuel, *of the tribe of Asher*. She was very old; she had lived with her husband seven years after her marriage, and then was a widow until she was eighty-four. She never left the temple but worshiped night and day, fasting and praying. Coming up to them at that very moment, she gave thanks to God and spoke about the child to all who were looking forward to the redemption of Jerusalem. (vv. 36–38, emphasis mine)

Anna, a descendant of the happy tribe of Asher, was privileged to see Him who had come to bless all the world with good tidings of great joy. Her aged eyes recognized the Christ child, and she gave thanks to God and spoke of the newborn Messiah to all who were looking for the redemption of Israel. She saw Him, embraced Him, explained Him to others, and became one of His first heralds.

How interesting that the biblical story of Asher is anchored by senior citizens who found strength in their latter years to fulfill their mission for the Lord:

- The aged Patriarch Jacob, whose deathbed blessing provided the framework of Asher's heritage.
- The venerable lawgiver Moses, whose final words set the course of Asher's history.

- The elderly Anna, whose greatest ministry occurred near the end of her life as she announced the first advent of the Messiah.

Jacob, Moses, Anna, Asher, and the tribe bearing his name—and you and me through Christ—are the recipients of a precious promise: "Your strength will equal your days."

ASHER'S LESSONS FOR US

That's the biblical story of the tribe of Asher, which gives us the background behind this great strength passage in Deuteronomy 33. As I studied verse 25 against this backdrop, I jotted down five lessons that encouraged me.

When we belong to Christ, we belong to a happy tribe. There's a sense in which we become honorary members of the tribe of Asher when we confess Jesus as Lord and believe in our hearts God has raised Him from the dead (Rom. 10:9–10). The Lord Jesus came to give abundant life, and only when we yield our hearts to Him can we tap into His joy. As Christ's followers we're appointed to live joyful lives and to bring a message of happiness to others. True happiness comes through a relationship with God via Christ; and once we know Him, we're obliged to live joyfully, for that reflects our Lord. Like Asher, we are most blessed—the happiest people on earth.

I wrote about this in my book *Mastering Life Before It's Too Late:*

God's very personality is full of joy. He is a God of joy. He is joyful in His essence and joyful by nature. He is joyful to the unfathomable core of His being. His character radiates joy like the sun radiating light, and it's impossible for us to experience genuine joy without conceptualizing the joyfulness of the Divine. . . .

Christians therefore have a sacred obligation to live joyfully. Joy is the duty of the Christian. According to Ecclesiastes 5:20, we should be "occupied with joy. . . ."[5]

The joy of the Lord is the only dynamic that enables us to keep moving forward at life's hardest moments. This kind of joy doesn't cancel the difficult moments of life, but it does transcend life's circumstances.[6]

Second, when we belong to Christ, He is our prosperity and protection. The Asherite region overflowed with olive oil, and the bolts of the gates of its cities were iron and bronze. Olive oil is a symbol in the Bible of the Holy Spirit and of joy, and bolts and gates are symbols of protection. When we belong to Christ, He is our prosperity and protection. He anoints our heads with oil and bathes our feet with joy. Romans 10:15 says, "How beautiful are the feet of those who bring good news." The Lord secures us within His protective gates of iron and bronze. Jesus said in John 10:9: "I am the gate; whoever enters through me will be saved. They will come in and go out, and find pasture."

We have enemies in life, the worst being Satan and his weapons of death and despair. He comes to steal, kill, and destroy. I was astonished the other day to read 1 John 5:19: "We know that we are children of God, and that the whole world is under the control of the evil one." Think of the implication of that sentence—the whole world is under Satan's control. The geo-political world. The world of entertainment. The world of academia. The world of finance. The worlds of philosophy and religion. The whole world is under the control of the evil one—except for those who are children of God through faith in Jesus Christ.

When you see the world tilting in a hellish direction, picture the safety of being protected within cross-shaped gates of iron and bronze. We're in the care of Him who said in His great prayer of John 17:15: "My prayer is not that you take them out of the world but that you protect them from the evil one."

Next, we have a Baby to introduce to the world. Just as the Bible's final reference to Asher is an announcement about Christ by aged Anna, so our great purpose on earth is to proclaim "Joy to the world! The Lord has come!" The Lord brings happiness to our hearts, gives us protection and prosperity, and commissions us as His ambassadors. He gives purpose to our earthly lives, and like Anna, we are to give thanks to God and speak about the Child to all who are looking forward to redemption.

Recently I've been thinking about how many people it takes—sometimes an entire church with everyone plying their gifts—to win others to Christ. It's not just one preacher, one evangelist, one invitation, one worship service, or one piece of literature.

Last Sunday I told my congregation in Nashville how Bill Bright, the evangelistic powerhouse who started Campus Crusade for Christ (now Cru), became a Christian as a young adult. Growing up in Oklahoma, he had wanted to become a rancher, get his law degree, own a newspaper, and run for public office. All that changed December 7, 1941, with Pearl Harbor. Bill was in college at the time, and he repeatedly tried to enlist in the armed forces but was rejected because of a perforated eardrum from a football injury.

He thought if he went to Los Angeles he might have a better chance of enlisting because of the volume of men pouring through the recruiting stations there. His mother, a dedicated Christian, packed a Bible into his belongings.

On his first night in Los Angeles, Bill picked up a hitchhiker who asked him where he was staying. Bill didn't have accommodations, and the hitchhiker invited him to stay where he was staying. It was with Dawson Trotman, the founder of the Navigators, who was zealous about winning and discipling young people for Christ.

A day or two later he tried to enlist in the military but again failed because of his eardrum. He eventually started his own business, selling specialty foods. He leased a room from an elderly couple who kept inviting him to Hollywood's First Presbyterian Church. One day he slipped into the back row of the church. The preacher was a good Bible teacher and Bill Bright found himself interested in the messages.

He soon received a phone call from a worker in the young adult division. She invited Bill to a party at the ranch of a movie star who attended the church. Bill agreed and that's how he began hanging around with a group of Christian singles. Eventually he began attending the young adult worship services on Wednesday nights, which were conducted by Dr. Henrietta Mears. Her Bible teaching began to create real interest in Bill about the Bible and about the gospel. He started making more friends. A lot of these young people gathered at the home of a man named Elwain Steinkamp, a real estate developer who built the prestigious Bel Air community. He made his large swimming pool available to the church.

One day beside the pool, Mr. Steinkamp said to Bill: "Material success is not where you find happiness. There are rich people all over this city who are the most miserable people you'll ever meet. Knowing and serving Jesus Christ is what's really important. He's the only way to find happiness." Then Mr. Steinkamp quoted the words of Jesus: "What does it profit a person if he gains the whole world but loses his own soul?"

That spoke to Bill, and he returned to his apartment and found the Bible his mother had packed for him. He began reading it. Several months passed, and one Wednesday night in the spring of 1945, Dr. Mears was teaching from Acts 22 on the conversion of Saul of Tarsus. She talked about Paul's two questions: "Who are you, Lord? What would you have me do?" Those are the most important questions we can ever ask, she said.

Bill returned to his apartment, knelt beside his bed, and gave his life to Jesus. Almost immediately he began winning others to Jesus. He poured himself into developing ways of reaching young adults and college students, and he went on to initiate some of the greatest evangelistic ministries the world has seen.

I shared that story with my church to show them it takes all of us working together to win people to Christ. In this case there was a whole cast of characters: a hitchhiker, a host who opened his home, a pastor, a Bible teacher, a set of landlords, a young lady on the phone, a young adult group, a movie star, a businessman with a swimming pool, and last but not least a mother who packed a Bible in her son's suitcase.

What happened there can happen with you and your church. We have the same God. We have the same purpose. Your city is filled with children, teens, young adults, and adults of all ages needing Christ. We cross paths with them every day, and as honorary members of the tribe of Asher we're given the joy of doing what Anna did during the first Christmas season—embracing Christ and announcing Him to the world. The Lord uses all of us as part of the process of fulfilling His mission.[7]

Paul made this point when he said in 1 Corinthians 3: "What, after all, is Apollos? And what is Paul? Only servants, through whom you came to believe—as the Lord has assigned to each his task. I planted the seed, Apollos watered it, but God has been making it grow" (vv 5–6).

Not all of us will play a starring role, and we may not see immediate results from our efforts; but God has assigned each of us a task in doing His work. He will give the increase—and that leads to my next observation.

The Lord promises us strength equal to our days. We'll never awaken to a morning in which the Lord has given us work to do or burdens to bear without providing the strength we need. We typically measure our lives in years; God measures our lives in terms of days. The earth revolves on its axis every twenty-four hours, giving us 365 new beginnings every year. The Bible says, "His compassions never fail. They are new every morning" (Lam. 3:22–23). The apostle Paul said, "Therefore we do not lose heart. Though outwardly we are wasting away, yet inwardly we are being renewed day by day" (2 Cor. 4:16). Jesus told us to take up our cross daily (Luke 9:23). God allots our work in one-day increments, and that's the only way we can tackle life.

Last year I visited Franklin D. Roosevelt's home in Hyde Park, New York, which is also the site of his presidential library. One of the displays is his original desk from the Oval Office, set up the way it was when he was president. It was so covered with equipment, papers, and knickknacks I wondered how he got anything done there. But the item that most intrigued me was a beautiful wooden frame. It didn't contain a picture of his wife or mother or children. At the top of the frame, the word "ENGAGEMENTS" was stamped in gold, and beneath the glass was the president's schedule for the day. It was called his "Appointments Easel," and every morning his daily agenda was slipped under the glass so he would know the plan for the day.

I believe God has an appointment easel set up in heaven for each of us, that He has a daily agenda for each of our lives. Psalm 139:16 says, "You saw me before I was born and scheduled each day of my life before I began to breathe. Every day was recorded in your book."[8] Stamped in stenciled letters across every day of our lives are the letters STRENGTH!

If we look at the immensity of the problems we face or the backlog of work towering over us like a mountain range, we'll break down. But everything changes when we realize we can't do yesterday's work or tomorrow's work or all the work. We can't solve yesterday's problems or tomorrow's problems or all the problems. We can simply do what God has assigned us today. Just for today we can do God's will, and just for today we'll have the needed strength to do the work and bear the load.

The promise in Deuteronomy 33:25 is that we'll have sufficient God-given strength for all our God-assigned tasks through each of our God-appointed days. Your strength will equal your days. And in God's providence, the final drops of our earthly strength in this life will perfectly correspond with the finishing of the work He has given us to do, and then we'll be taken up to heaven where we'll never know a weary day. Until then we can tap into God's enthusiasm without fearing inadequate internal resources. As Jesus taught us to pray "Give us this day our daily bread," so we can pray "Give us today our daily strength."

As I've studied the writings of earlier generations of Christians, I've come to realize how many heroes of the faith leaned heavily on Deuteronomy

33:25. The great preacher Charles Spurgeon, in a sermon based on this text, said: "The same God who guides the stars in their courses, who directs the earth in its orbit, who feeds the burning furnace of the sun, and keeps the stars perpetually burning with their fires—the same God has promised to supply thy strength. . . . As thy days, so shall thy strength be."[9]

About the same time Spurgeon preached his sermon on Deuteronomy 33:25, in the mid-1850s, a woman in Hawaii was clinging to the same verse for dear life. Her name was Lucy Thurston, and she was sixty. One day she found a tumor in her breast and was subsequently diagnosed with cancer. Her doctors advised her to consider immediate surgery, but they warned they couldn't use chloroform. The use of anesthesia was new, its side effects were unknown, and they were afraid to use it because Lucy had once battled a case of paralysis. She would be wide-awake during the surgery with nothing to dull the pain.

On the night before the operation, Lucy paced back and forth with a sense of helplessness and fear. But after praying and committing her fears to the Lord, as she later said, she was able to lay her head on the pillow and "sleep refreshingly." The next morning she awakened with a promise from God echoing in her heart—Deuteronomy 33:25.

"A bright day opened upon us," she later wrote to her daughter. "My feelings were natural, cheerful, elevated. I took the Lord at his own word: 'As thy day is, so shall thy strength be.' There with an unwavering heart, I leaned for strength and support."

Lucy's letter to her daughter is a remarkable document, almost a moment-by-moment description of what happened during her surgery, and I wouldn't advise reading it if you're faint of heart. Lucy recounted in bloody detail the entire procedure of undergoing a radical mastectomy, performed while wide-awake without anesthesia. But God gave her supernatural strength for the day and she was able to bear it. The surgery was a success and Lucy Thurston lived for another twenty-one years, finding God's strength sufficient in one-day allocations.[10]

I can't imagine what Lucy endured; but none of us knows what any given day will bring, and sometimes we have to face life without anesthesia. Life can change in a moment, and every day is filled with emergencies, stresses, distresses, and disasters. At the same time, every day holds the promise of work, labor, purpose, success, and fulfillment. As children of God, we have a promise in Deuteronomy 33:25 with no cutoffs, letups, lapses, or hindrances: God will give you the strength to complete any task He assigns or to bear any burden He allows, for as our days, shall our strength ever be.

Elisabeth Elliot warns against worrying too much about tomorrow, for, she says: "The future is not our province. . . . We are meddling with God's business when we let all manner of imaginings loose, predicting disaster, contemplating possibilities instead of following, one day at a time, God's plain and simple pathway. . . . 'As thy days, so shall thy strength be' was Moses' blessing for Asher—in other words, your strength will equal your days. God knows how to apportion each one's strength according to that day's need, however great or small."[11]

Finally, don't forget that beneath us are the everlasting arms. As Moses wrapped up his final message to the nation of Israel, he ended with one of the most powerful images that ever flowed from his lips: "Your strength will equal your days. There is no one like the God of Jeshurun, who rides across the heavens to help you and on the clouds in His majesty. The eternal God is your refuge, and underneath are the everlasting arms."

I like the way Patricia Knight puts this in her book, *Pure Joy.* "No matter what the Lord chooses as your assignment for each day," she wrote, "He will also provide the strength. 'Your strength will equal your days.' And then, if a situation becomes too tough, 'the eternal God is your refuge and underneath are the everlasting arms.'"[12]

I wonder what comes to your mind when picturing that phrase. I used to think of this image in terms of high trapeze artists flying through the air, missing their grip, and plunging into the net below. It's easy for me to visualize Deuteronomy 33:25 in that way. When we lose our grip on life, we fall—but only into the safety net of the Lord's everlasting arms.

But Moses had never been to a circus. He had been a shepherd, and earlier in Deuteronomy 1:29–31, he said: "Do not be terrified; do not be afraid. . . . The LORD your God, who is going before you, will fight for you, as he did for you in Egypt, before your very eyes, and in the wilderness. There you saw how the LORD your God carried you, as a father carries his son, all the way you went until you reached this place."

Earlier this year as I hiked with a friend in the Dolomites, we came across a newborn lamb that had fallen into a narrow crevice. In struggling to get out, it had buried itself more deeply in the unyielding rock, becoming hopelessly stuck. The flies had gathered, and the little lamb had given up and was dying. It was so squeezed into the fissure it couldn't move a muscle. We heaved a rock out of the way, and I lifted the lamb out of the cranny—out of its cesspool of manure and urine—slid my arms under its belly, pressed it against my chest, and carried it down the hill to reunite it with the flock. There was an occasional bleat, but he seemed to know he was secure in my arms. This is the picture Moses had in mind when he said ". . . and underneath are the everlasting arms."

Sometimes we feel we're stuck in a depression or abyss. We're in a jam. We're squeezed into a fissure that's trying to squeeze out our faith. We grow discouraged. Perhaps even now you feel like giving up.

This is the time to remember the promise of Asher. When you belong to Jesus, you belong to a happy tribe. He is your prosperity and protection. He bathes your feet in the oil of His Spirit. He is your message of joy for the world, and He apportions strength for each day. As Isaiah said, "He gathers the lambs in his arms and carries them close to his heart" (Isa. 40:11).

As long as you live, God will keep His promise to impart sufficient strength for the work He assigns and the burdens He allows. Tap into His endless current of divine energy. His promise, "Your strength will equal your days," is a high voltage line of Scripture, and you can connect to it now.

A WORD FROM KATRINA

I grew up in a Finnish home in Maine, moved to Florida, and then to South Carolina, where I met Robert in college in 1973. We were married in 1976, began pastoring in 1977, and have raised three daughters.

In the late 1980s, I began having strange sensations in my extremities—a burning feeling and numbness of hands and feet. I recall stretching out on the floor so Rob and the girls could pull at my hands and feet because somehow that relieved my discomfort. As I walked through our community every day for exercise, my legs developed a funny feeling. One day at the airport they stopped working altogether. I was stranded in the concourse, unable to move. Shortly thereafter, in 1990, I was diagnosed with multiple sclerosis.

Today I'm confined to a wheelchair. Every morning as Rob lifts me out of bed and into the bathroom, the weakness is the same. It never gets better. But I've learned to remember Deuteronomy 33:25 and let it determine my mindset. It's very practical to me because it reminds me God's strength is proportional to each day's challenge. I've never had a day when the power supply from this verse was interrupted. I don't always have a lot of strength, but I have sufficient strength for what's required. You will too.

As my days, so shall my strength be.

TWO

Turn Messes into Momentum

The eyes of the LORD range throughout the earth to
strengthen those whose hearts are fully committed to him.

2 CHRONICLES 16:9

Missionary biography is my favorite genre of inspirational reading. Here we find accounts of truly unforgettable characters—like Lucy Thurston in the prior chapter—who found themselves in unbelievable situations, often in danger, doing the world's greatest work on the front lines for the kingdom. These are the stories that encourage me to do more and to do better.[1]

On a recent vacation, I devoured an old paperback autobiography of Mabel Francis, an American worker who sailed to Japan in 1909, sent by the Christian and Missionary Alliance. She labored there through World War I, through the Great Depression, and in the difficult years leading up to World War II. She was in her sixties when the Japanese attacked Pearl Harbor. Mabel decided to stay in Japan and continue her work as best she could during the war. She wanted to be there after the conflict—whoever won or lost—to spread the healing message of the gospel in a postwar era.

As the war worsened, Mabel was placed under house arrest in her Tokyo home. Over the years, she had won the respect of the local police and governmental officials, and they treated her with humanity. In return Mabel turned her home into a sort of small hospital and tended the sick who came to her. But finally the day came when she was interred in a wartime prison camp, which was housed in a large building in Tokyo. Though never mistreated, Mabel's deteriorating conditions were lonely, sparse, and frightening. The food became worse and worse, and some days there was none at all.

Toward the end of the war another danger arose. The Allies began bombing Tokyo, and every night she heard the droning of B-29s in the skies over Japan. The explosions came closer and closer. One night a bomb destroyed an adjacent building and the fire spread. The prisoners were herded into the streets where they huddled in the open air with flames all around them, surrounded by suffering people, orphaned children, weeping women, and broken men. Mosquitoes tormented them.

In her autobiography, Mabel described the difficulties of those days. The whole city was in ruins. She was weakened, undernourished, and exhausted, and she faced unbelievable suffering on every side. With no money, she was desperate and destitute. That's when Mabel opened her Bible and found a single verse that stayed with her the rest of her life. It was a verse about personal strength, about physical, mental, spiritual, moral, and emotional stamina. It was 2 Chronicles 16:9.

In her book, she wrote:

> Then, God gave me the promise of Second Chronicles 16:9: "The eyes of the LORD run to and fro throughout the whole earth, to show himself strong in the behalf of them whose heart is perfect toward him."
>
> "The eyes of the Lord . . . ." He knows just where the money is and

where our help is coming from. This was to be our source of strength all through those days, as one miracle followed another.[2]

The rest of Mabel's book tells about the indelible ministry she conducted in postwar Japan—the open doors and the incredible things that happened through her. She teamed up with the Japanese pastor of the First Methodist Church, located in Ginza, the main street of Tokyo. The church had a big hole in its roof because of a bomb, but that turned out to be a blessing. Every night the church sponsored gospel concerts and the music rang out through the hole, spread over the center of the city, and drew people in.

American GIs flooded Japan, and many were zealous Christians. Mabel recruited them to do a tremendous work in Tokyo and beyond. A series of programs called the GI Gospel Hour became the means of many Japanese citizens coming to Christ, and it led to the founding of Far Eastern Gospel Crusade. Today it's known as SEND International, sponsoring about six hundred missionaries in more than twenty nations in Asia and elsewhere.[3]

Mabel also went down to Hiroshima and led people to Christ who had survived the atomic bomb. She helped organize a church among the survivors. After the very first service when nearly everyone was gone, Mabel noticed a little woman standing at the side who seemed to want to say something. Mabel took her hand and asked her to sit and talk. "The morning when the bomb struck," said the woman, "I was at my home, up on the mountainside. My two little children were playing on the floor—a one-year-old and a three-year-old. I stooped down to pick up something, and in that second, that awful flash of light came! I was startled, and stood up to look around, and when I looked back, my two children were charred at my feet—both dead. I didn't know then that I was all burned, I was so concerned for my little ones. I picked them up and laid them aside, and pretty soon I began to feel the pain in my own body. Then I found how badly I was burned."

The woman went on to tell Mabel of her overwhelming despair, her suffering, and her attempts to drag herself to every shrine and every temple, looking for peace, but nothing helped. "But tonight you told us of this God's love, and that it was He who created us, and you said my children are with Him—I believe it! I believe it! My heart is comforted. Light has come to me."[4]

In this way, Mabel, with unflagging energy, brought hope and healing to the only nation in history decimated by a nuclear attack. When she finally left Japan in her old age, the entire country owed her a debt of gratitude. She was recognized as an honorary citizen of her city and honored for her lifetime of service, which was accomplished in the strength of the Lord.

Her secret, as she always said afterward, was the promise of 2 Chronicles 16:9: "For the eyes of the LORD range throughout the earth to strengthen those whose hearts are fully committed to him."

This very same promise is as available to us now as it was in biblical times or during the days of World War II. It's for you and me just as surely as it applied to Mabel or any other missionary. It's a promise with no geographical limitations. It's a promise of strength with no expiration date. It has no shelf life; it's perpetually fresh and potent. The eyes of the Lord never droop, never close, never slumber, and never sleep. Every moment of every day our Lord's eagle eye scans every corner of the globe, surveying every heart of every person, looking for someone, for you, for anyone whose heart is fully committed to Jesus Christ. He gives us strength to turn our messes into momentum and our battles into victories.

For the eyes of the LORD range throughout the earth to strengthen those whose hearts are fully committed to Him.

ASA'S FIRST CHAPTER

This is a wonderful stand-alone verse; but of course, it doesn't stand alone. It has a context. It's woven into a dramatic story in the Bible involving one of the colorful kings of ancient Judah—Asa, who reigned in Jerusalem forty-one years. We can best understand the promise by seeing it in situ, and that involves a three-chapter study of the Bible. The story of King Asa occupies three consecutive chapters in 2 Chronicles.

The first chapter—2 Chronicles 14—tells how he started off. According to 2 Chronicles 14:1, Asa advanced to the throne of Judah upon the death of his father, King Abijah. For ten years thereafter, all went well. The young man confronted no enemies and fought no wars. He "did what was good and right in the eyes of the LORD his God. He removed the foreign altars and the high places, smashed the sacred stones and cut down the Asherah poles" (vv. 2–3). These poles were Canaanite fertility symbols that may have featured images of the female goddess Asherah. Asa destroyed the idols and sought to cleanse the land of idolatry and bring revival to Judah.

A nation is blessed when it has godly leaders who understand the moral baseline of right and wrong as revealed in the Judeo-Christian principles of Scripture. In America, that heritage seems nearly gone now; but 2 Chronicles is the Bible's manual on revival, and I'm still holding out hope (and praying) for a revival in our world today.

In promoting revival in his own day, Asa "commanded Judah to seek the LORD, the God of their ancestors, and to obey His laws and commands. He removed the high places and incense altars in every town in Judah, and the kingdom was at peace under him. He built up the fortified cities of Judah, since the land was at peace. No one was at war with him during those years, for the LORD gave him rest" (2 Chron. 14:4–6).

For the first ten years of his reign, the nation of Judah enjoyed peace and prosperity under a young king whose life and leadership displayed a touch from God. But troubles come sooner or later, and almost without warning a powerful enemy threw down the gauntlet and threatened Judah with sudden and genocidal destruction. Word arrived of a great invasion force of a million men swarming up from Africa, intent on overwhelming and conquering the nation of Judah. Though Asa had a large army—about a half-million men—he was still outnumbered two to one, and his military prospects were bleak.

These are the moments that demand strength, and this is sometimes where my strength fails. My initial response to a crisis is intense fear and a desperate attempt to hold myself together. I've had middle-of-the-night phone calls bringing dreaded news. I've awakened to find my house on fire, gotten news of terrible wrecks involving my kids, and had other experiences that have turned my hair gray; but I've also panicked at smaller things—a basement flooding, a passport missing, an animal running away, a child out too late, an airplane in turbulence.

Oh, how we need daily strength to face the problems—large and small—that jump out at us like jack-in-the-boxes.

The Bible doesn't tell us exactly where Asa was when he heard the dreaded news of the coming invasion, but we know how he responded. Some people would have emotionally collapsed, and perhaps Asa was rattled at first. But he resolved to trust in God 100 percent. Without wavering, without faintheartedness, Asa "called to the LORD his God and said, 'LORD, there is no one like you to help the powerless against the mighty. Help us, LORD our God, for we rely on you, and in your name we have come against this vast army. LORD, you are our God; do not let mere mortals prevail against you'" (2 Chron. 14:11).

The Lord responded to the king's prayer and to his faith. Against all odds, Judah routed the enemy, and their victory is described in the remainder of the chapter. Whenever I read this chapter, I want to pray for a faith like Asa's. Hymnist William H. Bathurst put it into song:

O, for a faith that will not shrink, though pressed by every foe,
That will not tremble on the brink of any earthly woe![5]

ASA'S SECOND CHAPTER

The second chapter of Asa's life is given in 2 Chronicles 15, when, after his resounding victory over the African forces, a preacher paid him a visit.

Anytime we have a great victory we're in danger of pride, apathy, and the ravages of fatigue. So as soon as things settled down, God did something wonderful for Asa. He sent him a prophet named Azariah to remind him and his countrymen to renew their commitment to God. We know nothing about this prophet, Azariah, except what we read in this chapter. He's one of the Bible's so-called minor characters, but on this occasion he had a timely message.

> The Spirit of God came on Azariah son of Oded. He went out to meet Asa
> and said to him, "Listen to me, Asa and all Judah and Benjamin. The LORD
> is with you when you are with him. If you seek him, he will be found by
> you, but if you forsake him, he will forsake you. For a long time Israel was
> without the true God, without a priest to teach and without the law. But in
> their distress they turned to the LORD, the God of Israel, and sought him,
> and he was found by them. In those days it was not safe to travel about, for
> all the inhabitants of the lands were in great turmoil. One nation was being
> crushed by another and one city by another, because God was troubling
> them with every kind of distress. But as for you, be strong and do not give
> up, for your work will be rewarded." (2 Chron. 15:1–7)

Asa drank in the words and embraced this message as if God were truly speaking it to him and to his people. Verse 8 says that on hearing this sermon the king "took courage." Perhaps the strain of the crisis had drained his emotions, but a word from the Lord restored his passion for progress. When a destabilizing crisis comes and goes, we need the truths of God to restabilize our minds and restore our spirits. Asa rejoiced in the fresh message from God, and the rest of the chapter describes how he initiated another revival movement, extending the message of the Lord to newly acquired territories.

He also convened a great assembly in Jerusalem, summoning people from every corner of his kingdom. Asa led his nation in renewing their covenant to God. The last part of the chapter tells us Asa even deposed his own grandmother—the Queen Mother of Judah—because she refused to destroy her idols to serve the Lord unswervingly. Asa was a man of vast military, political, and spiritual strength, popular with his people. He ruled in peace and prosperity and with a sense of national pride and purpose. He's an example to us of how God blesses a nation, an organization, a church, or a family whose leadership honors Him. Crises may arise and tough times may come, but in Him we have the resources to keep us going from strength to strength.

ASA'S THIRD CHAPTER

If the story ended there, King Asa would have gone down as one of the greatest kings in history. But, alas, the story doesn't end there. We have a third and final chapter of Scripture devoted to this man—2 Chronicles 16. Inexplicably, the Bible passes silently over the next quarter-century and picks up the story in Asa's latter days, in the thirty-fifth year of his reign. To our surprise and disappointment, the man changed. His disciplines eroded. His spirituality corroded and crumbled. He no longer listened to the preaching of the prophets, and he no longer trusted God with the crises of life. He himself needed a personal revival, but he'd grown disinterested.

According to 2 Chronicles 16, in the thirty-fifth year of his tenure, Asa faced another threat—this time on his northern flanks. Rather than rely on God for guidance and protection, he entered a military alliance with Syria, using silver and gold from the treasuries of the Lord's temple to seal the deal. At first glance, this may seem a logical move. Faced with threats from the Northern Kingdom of Israel, King Asa appeared to be moving his pieces adroitly on the chessboard of the Middle East. But it was wrong. It was a reversal, a disaster.

Asa raided the temple of Jehovah, took the silver and gold and the vessels and the treasures of the temple, and he used God's holy instruments to bribe a godless nation to save him in a crisis. Asa didn't pray. He didn't seek the Lord. He didn't call his people to repentance or revival. He didn't proclaim a national day of fasting and prayer. Caught up in the geopolitics of the moment, he commandeered God's sacred vessels to induce the Syrian government to come to his defense.

That's when another preacher showed up, a prophet named Hanani, who minced no words, telling him: "Because you relied on the king of Aram [Syria] and not on the LORD your God, the army of the king of Aram has escaped from your hand. Were not the Cushites and Libyans a mighty army with great numbers of chariots and horsemen? Yet when you relied on the LORD, He delivered them into your hand" (verses 7–8).

That brings us to our verse 9: "For the eyes of the Lord range throughout the earth to strengthen those whose hearts are fully committed to him. You have done a foolish thing, and from now on you will be at war."

Asa responded bitterly, throwing the prophet into prison. At the same time he brutally oppressed some of his people, probably those most loyal to the Lord. In the aftermath, Asa lost his footing—literally. Verses 12–13 say: "In the thirty-ninth year of his reign, Asa was afflicted with a disease in his feet. Though his disease was severe, even in his illness he did not seek help from the LORD, but only from the physicians. Then in the forty-first year of his reign Asa died. . . ."

Even as I retell this story, I feel heartbroken. I don't know how to explain it. How can a man be a spiritual leader in his nation, bring about revival, trust God in times of crisis, and then, late in his life, mess up so completely he turned away from the Lord and ended as a failure? I do not understand it, but I know it happens. It happens all the time. It can happen to any of us.

When I yielded my life to the Lord as a college student in the dormitory at Columbia International University in 1971, a classmate from across the hall mentored me. Joe took a tremendous interest in helping me grow spiritually. I'd never met anyone like this fellow. He was aflame for the Lord as if drenched with kerosene. He led me through the Navigator *Design for*

Discipleship Bible studies, and his zeal and teaching left a lasting impact on my life.

Joe had once been a gang member in New York City, but he had been converted in North Carolina and taken in by Billy and Ruth Graham. They spent many hours with him. There in the dormitory, Joe taught me everything Ruth had taught him. On several occasions he took me to see her at the Graham home in North Carolina, and my visits with her were unforgettable.

Joe and I graduated together in 1974 and went our separate ways. Occasionally I heard disturbing things about him. There was evidently some kind of relapse, some kind of spiritual reversal or downturn. I knew Ruth was worried about him too. I tried to reconnect with him a time or two, but things weren't the same. A couple of years ago, I felt a burden to find him again, to track him down, to see how he was doing. I talked to a mutual friend and said, "Do you have Joe's address and phone number?"

"I'm sorry to tell you this," said my friend, "but Joe is dead."

It was like a stab in my heart, and it's one of the mysteries and sorrows of my life. I don't know what happened. I cannot explain it. But I know even the apostle Paul was worried that something similar could happen to him, that he could mess up near the finish line, that he could lose his effectiveness and testimony. He told the Corinthians he worked every day to keep his body under discipline "so that after I have preached to others, I myself will not be disqualified for the prize" (1 Cor. 9:27).

This was the danger addressed by the prophet Hanani, when he spoke the words of 2 Chronicles 16:9: "For the eyes of the LORD range throughout the earth to strengthen those whose hearts are fully committed to him."

ASA'S LESSONS FOR US

How can we avoid Asa's mistake? How can we make sure our hearts remain fully committed to Jesus Christ all our lives?

First, use every significant occasion in life to rededicate yourself to Christ. The Bible says, "He died for all, that those who live should no longer live for themselves but for him who died for them and was raised again" (2 Cor. 5:15). Our Christian lives have a distinct beginning when we decide to follow Jesus. When we confess our need for a Savior and acknowledge the risen Christ as our Lord, at that moment we are redeemed; we are saved; we are born again; we are heaven bound. That's a decision we don't need to repeat. We are saved once for all. But along the way, we have many opportunities to reaffirm that decision, to deepen it, and to rededicate ourselves to the Lord.

That's what Peter did by the Sea of Galilee in John 21 when he expressed his love for Jesus three times and was reinstated to his life's calling. That's what Thomas did when he proclaimed to Christ, "My Lord and my God!" (John 20:28). That's what David did in Psalm 51 after repenting of his sin.

That's what Samuel did in 1 Samuel 7. In this passage, Samuel led the Israelites to a military conquest over the Philistines. When the people assembled later to celebrate their victory, Samuel had a large stone erected between the towns of Mizpah and Shen. He gave the monument a name: Ebenezer, which is a Hebrew term meaning "Stone of Help." Samuel told the people, "Thus far the LORD has helped us" (v. 12). It was a physical reminder for the people to acknowledge God's blessings in the past and, by implication, to maintain their dedication to Him for the future.

We need to go through life raising Ebenezers and using every significant life event to rededicate ourselves to God and to say, "Thus far has the LORD helped me."

- On New Year's Day, say, "Lord, You've helped me all my life. Here at the beginning of another year, I rededicate myself to Jesus."
- On your birthday, say, "Lord, another year is past; I rededicate myself for the time remaining for me on earth."
- When you graduate from school, when you begin a career, when

you marry your sweetheart, when a child is born, spend some time alone before God and recommit yourself to Him.

- When a crisis is faced or finished, we can learn its lessons and resolve to live more fully by faith every day as those "who with unveiled faces contemplate the Lord's glory" and "are being transformed into His image with ever-increasing glory" (2 Cor. 3:18).
- When a prayer is answered, when a loved one dies, when a tragedy occurs, when a victory is won, rededicate yourself to Christ.
- When we move into a new house, when we start a new job, when we're given a promotion, when we retire from our field of labor, use it as an occasion to look backward with gratitude and look forward with renewed faith.

I happened to be at a conference in Chicago many years ago when I turned thirty-five. Sometime during the day—I don't recall whether it was morning or afternoon—I took a long walk along the lakefront and found a little private grove of bushes and trees. There I knelt down and prayed. I said, "Lord, I am thirty-five years old today. If I live the biblical three-score-and-ten, this is the halfway point in my life. You have led me thus far, but I want to rededicate myself for the years that remain." Though decades ago, I still remember the "hallowedness" of that moment.

If we raise Ebenezers along the way, when we get to the end of life we'll look back and see a long series of stone markers, twisting with our pathway, elevated heavenward, marking our moments of reaffirmation and the renewal of our vows to Him.

> Here I raise my Ebenezer;
> Hither by Thy help I've come;
> And I hope, by Thy good pleasure,
> Safely to arrive at home.[6]

At some point, King Asa forgot all about raising Ebenezers. He fell into apathy and lost his commitment to God.

We must also keep listening to sound biblical teaching. Asa listened and responded to every word of the prophet Azariah when he was young. But a quarter-century later, he had no patience with the prophet Hanani. He lost his appetite for God's Word. I'm certain he had stopped reading the Scripture personally. Maybe he got busy. Maybe he became distracted. Maybe something disappointed or embittered him. But somehow, somewhere, Asa drifted away from the daily study of Scripture.

We need to keep a watertight seal around our minds. Today's society is essentially atheistic, which means people are operating with the assumption there are no moral guidelines from an absolute source. I'm not an atheist, because I know I cannot disprove the existence of God universally and perpetually. I'm not an agnostic, for it's illogical to believe in the possibility of a God who does not have the ability or the desire to communicate. I believe, in the words of Francis Schaeffer, He is there and He is not silent.[7] The Creator has given me a book small enough to hold in my hands, large enough to study for a lifetime, and rich enough to satisfy my mind and heart forever. If our greatest joy in life is our daily fellowship with God in His Word and prayer, we'll never tire of His teaching, reject His authority, or lose His blessings on our lives.

In his book, *Daily Rituals: How Artists Work*, Mason Currey studied the routines of a wide array of creative people. He found everyone needs a workable daily routine to be productive. He wrote in his introduction: "A solid routine fosters a well-worn groove for one's mental energies and helps stave off the tyranny of moods. This was one of William James's favorite subjects. He thought you wanted to put part of your life on autopilot; by forming good habits, he said, we can 'free our minds to advance to really interesting fields of action.'"[8]

I love thinking in those terms. When we have a regular daily ritual or routine, it provides the grooves through which our productivity is channeled and our work is done. It supplies the furrows in which we can work, rest, raise our families, order our lives, and renew our energy. For the Christian, the daily ritual of Bible study and prayer is the most important part of our routine. Added to that is our weekly routine of attending church and soaking in the preached and taught Word.[9]

King Asa somehow got away from loving the Law of God. He missed a day, then a week, then a month. He neglected to attend worship at the temple. He got busy with other things, and he thought he could just rest on past spiritual experiences. His daily walk with the Lord was crowded out of his schedule. That is absolutely deadly, and if it's happening to you or me, we need to snap out of it now.

Third, don't quit before the finish line. I've never been an athlete, but when I was in high school I tried running. My biggest problem was the temptation to let up my speed as I approached the finish line. As soon as I saw I was near the tape, I would slack off a little. My coaches could never cure me of that; I don't know why. But I don't want to do the same thing in life. I want to keep going to the end. Our pace may indeed change; the location of the track may alter with time. But we don't want to quit before finishing the race before us. We want to play to the whistle.

Finally, claim 2 Chronicles 16:9 for yourself. In these days of stress and strain, we need strength of body, mind, soul, and spirit. We need strength sufficient for each day's work, for each month's journey, for each year's challenges. We need strength against sorrow, against temptation, against fatigue, against discouragement. We need to be stronger people as we tackle life for all it's worth. We need to build momentum and pick up speed.

Asa had a long reign punctuated by two messy situations. He turned the first mess into spiritual momentum that inspired his nation, but later he turned his momentum into a mess and ended his story in misfortune and misery.

When we're spiritually anemic, we're weak in every other way. But when we're strong in spirit, we tap into the omnipotence of our almighty God and find daily strength for daily needs.

As I worked on this chapter, I had supper in the home of a retired missionary named Monie Motis, who served in nations like Liberia and Eritria. As we talked about this verse, she excused herself, went to a back room in her house, and returned with a little stack of 4 x 6 index cards covered with typing and wrapped in a rubber band. These were the Bible memory verses she had selected and typed years ago. She had worked on memorizing the passages and over the years had committed them all to memory, although she still takes them with her on walks in her neighborhood in Sebring, Florida, and reviews them.

She told me these verses got her through the ordeal of being held hostage in Liberia during a critical time. And these verses were the only thing she was able to take with her when she was released and fled the country. Later, in Eritrea, a friend of hers came to see her. He was a Christian young man and a member of the Eritrean Armed Forces.

He said, "Mrs. Motis, when the Ethiopians invaded, I saw them coming and it was like a long, wide, endless green river rolling toward us. I was exhausted and frightened and didn't know how I could rest. But I remembered you were praying for me, and so I slid down into my foxhole and was able to sleep. Will you please continue praying for me?"

Monie was overwhelmed with the responsibility of the request. Looking into his eyes, she wanted to say or do something to strengthen him as long as he lived. Taking her precious stack of index cards, she selected one and gave it to the soldier. It was 2 Chronicles 16:9: "For the eyes of the LORD range throughout the earth to strengthen those whose hearts are fully committed to him."

When he left her house, he was clutching that card as a parting gift and as a precious heritage.

"Did you replace the card in your stack?" we asked Monie. "Did you type it up again and replace it in your cards?"

"I didn't need to," she replied. "When I returned to the States a friend in South Dakota, who knew nothing of those events, gave me a gift. I'll show it to you." Leading us to the kitchen, she took a ceramic plaque from above the sink. It was a beautiful colorful rendition of 2 Chronicles 16:9. "The Lord made sure I kept this verse before my eyes and in my heart," she said.

The Bible tells us to post Scriptures around our houses ("Write them on the doorframes of your houses and on your gates"—Deuteronomy 6:9). Here's a verse to anchor to the walls of your mind and memory. Make sure to keep it before your eyes and heart too, and practice it. Tap into it. Use it to build yourself up, to gain momentum with the passing years, and to turn messes into momentum.

For the eyes of the LORD range throughout the earth to strengthen those whose hearts are fully committed to him.

A WORD FROM KATRINA

My multiple sclerosis is causing me more problems than ever before, perhaps because I am getting older. Just last night, I knocked everything off my bedside table, and I couldn't retrieve them—glasses, phone, cough drops, book, flashlight. It's the little things that do me in. Being pushed down the sidewalk with my feet flying off the footpads is very frustrating to me. We try to avoid cobblestones at all costs. Going to restaurants isn't a treat anymore, or eating in public. I'm quite awkward with my utensils. And oh, that disheveled look. I have a hard time feeling presentable.

But being handicapped is no excuse for unfaithfulness because the Lord prizes loyalty. Loyalty is faithfulness all the time—no pity parties or days off. I'm to be holy as He is holy (1 Peter 1:16). I don't want to be lacking when He looks my way. "For the eyes of the Lord run to and fro throughout the whole earth, to show Himself strong on behalf of those whose heart is loyal to Him (NKJV)."

This verse promises strength; that strength is *Christ in me, the hope of glory!* (Col. 1:27).

THREE

Invest in a Power Company

The joy of the Lord is your strength.

When it comes to electric power—things like lights and generators—history gives a lot of credit to Thomas A. Edison, but he didn't do it all. The last half of the 1800s teemed with hundreds of inventors and innovators. Near the top of the list was Charles F. Brush, who was born on a farm near Cleveland in 1849. He began tinkering with science and electricity in childhood, and by age twelve he'd built his own static electric machine. In high school he constructed an arc light. Borrowing money from an uncle, he enrolled in the University of Michigan and graduated in a mere two years. He found a job with a mining company, but every spare moment was given to experimenting with electricity.

In 1876 while vacationing back on the family farm, he put a horse on a treadmill and used its energy to generate electricity. Talk about horsepower! Out of the experience Brush developed and patented a magnetoelectric machine. He also invented commercial lighting by developing an arc lamp that could be installed and illuminated by the electricity generated from his machine.[1]

In the spring of 1879, months before Edison switched on his light bulb, Brush erected a series of tall poles topped with lights around the public square in downtown Cleveland. Just before eight o'clock on the evening of April 29, he activated the power. The lamp closest to the Telegraph Supply Company flickered, the lights came on, and suddenly the night was illumined like magic. The crowd cheered, the local band burst into a rousing march, and artillery on the lakeshore boomed in honor of the event.[2]

It was just the beginning. He went on to light up city after city in America. It was Brush, not Edison, who created the "Great White Way" by installing electric lights up and down Broadway two full years before Edison opened his New York Power Plant.[3]

Some of Brush's fiercest critics were the executives of municipal gas companies, who feared electric lights would put them out of business. But Brush tapped down their objections by explaining how electric lights in public areas would increase gas lighting in private homes. His words almost have a spiritual ring to them:

> People have been living in darkness so long that they have organized their lives on that basis. But when they get used to light, they are sure to want more of it. After seeing brilliantly lighted streets and stores, they'll want more light in their homes and will burn more gas. As they use more gas for lighting, you can make gas cheaper and that will open up almost limitless industrial uses.[4]

Brush's words have a striking application to our personalities. People today have been living in the darkness so long they've organized their lives on that basis. They've lived with low wattage so long they've forgotten what it's like to operate at full power. Some of us have been living dimly, weakly, flickeringly, when God wants us to shine. We've been dragging ourselves through life when God wants us to run vigorously and rigorously. When we begin to realize we have endless sources of renewable energy available to us, we'll want it more and more. When we experience the light, we'll want to walk in it all the time. We need to organize our lives in the light.

What we need, then, is an electrical generator within us, producing energy for each day's responsibilities. We need an internal source of limitless power. But where do we find a generator like that? How can we install a power plant in our hearts?

Welcome to the 810 Power Company, which offers heat and light for the interior of our souls without ever sending a monthly bill. I'm talking about Nehemiah 8:10, a little verse offering eight dramatic words, into which you can invest your life:

The joy of the LORD is your strength.

In this passage, the Bible describes divine joy as a sort of internal generator activated by the Holy Spirit to produce all the energy and strength we need for a happy and holy life. The joy of the Lord gives us vim, vigor, vitality, and endurance. When God pumps His endless supply of joy into our systems, we find zest and zeal for whatever life brings.

There is an essential and undeniable relationship between joy and strength. Imagine, for example, you're sitting on a park bench, nursing your coffee and resting from a long walk. For entertainment, you engage in studying the people scurrying to and fro on the sidewalks. On the shady side of the street you see a person who's visibly despondent. There's no smile on his face. Hands stuffed into pockets. Shoulders slumped. Expression grim. Over on the sunny side of the street, someone is visibly happy. She's smiling. Looking up. Admiring the weather.

Which person do you think has the most energy?

Take another glance at them. Do you see what's slung over the shoulder of the depressed person? It's a gym bag and he's just finished his workout, though it probably wasn't one of his better ones. He's lean and muscular. He's in great shape. He is free from disease or disability. On the other hand, the person on the sunny side of the street has been sick for weeks and she's walking with the aid of a cane. You can tell she's in pain because of her limp and an occasional involuntary grimace.

Still, which one of these two people has the most energy? Which is ready to tackle the day? Which has resilience? It's the person with the most joy. Discouragement saps our energy; joy restores it. There's a direct link between our spirit and our spunk. If the generator of joy is humming away in our hearts, it relays strength to every fiber of our being. We feel its effects emotionally, physically, and spiritually. However weak we may be in bodily strength, the powerhouse of joy sends stamina into our hearts, bringing light to our eyes and a glow to our faces.

Discouragement short-circuits our vibrancy, making even small tasks seem impossible. I sometimes like to remind myself that all discouragement is from the devil; all encouragement is from the Lord. The joy of the Lord is what gives us strength. The joy of the Lord *is* our strength.

How did that verse—Nehemiah 8:10—find its way into God's Word? As we saw with Deuteronomy 33 and 2 Chronicles 16, our favorite verses on strength are best appreciated by knowing when, how, why, and to whom they were given. God hasn't given us a book simply filled with miscellaneous quotations or motivational mottos. He has given us a book rich in history, with riveting plots, unforgettable characters, and enriching stories. Every great quotation has a great context.

In this case, the context is the book of Nehemiah, which tells the story of an effective leader whose major role in Scripture was rebuilding the broken-down walls around Jerusalem several hundred years before the birth of Christ. It's the Bible's manual on leadership and project management, and it can arguably be called the greatest leadership book ever written.

It's also a great book about traveling the pilgrim pathway, going from strength to strength. The word "strength" occurs four times in Nehemiah, and the whole story of the rebuilding of the walls can be hung on those four references.

GOD'S STRENGTH IS GREAT—NEHEMIAH 1:10

The story opens in chapter 1, when Nehemiah was serving in the court of King Artaxerxes in the palace in Susa (in modern-day Iran). Like Daniel and Esther, Nehemiah was a God-fearing Jew who providentially advanced to a position of high responsibility in the Persian Empire. One day a delegation of friends showed up in Susa. They had traveled nearly a thousand miles from Jerusalem—the Holy City, the city of God's presence—which had been reduced to ruins. After the Babylonian invasion, Jerusalem was largely abandoned until a remnant of Jews returned to resettle the land and rebuild a modest version of the Jewish Temple (see Ezra 1–6). The remnant was hanging on by a thread, but Nehemiah's heart was with them. So when the visitors showed up in Susa, Nehemiah was full of questions. How were they doing? What's the news from Jerusalem?

What he learned was devastating. "It's a disaster," said the travelers.[5] The remnant was discouraged and intimidated by their enemies. The ancient walls of the city were in ruins. The people had no way of protecting themselves. Jerusalem was defenseless, and the returning Jews were at risk. The local population didn't want them there. The rebuilding effort was underfunded, and without walls there would be no restored Jewish capital. The dream of resettling the Holy Land and restoring the nation of Israel was at risk. God's promises hung in the balance, and all could have been lost for lack of walls and gates.

Nehemiah's heart was broken and a deep burden came over him. He could hardly eat or sleep, so great was his concern for the future of God's work in the place he loved. He fasted, prayed, confessed his sin and those of his people, and sought guidance from God. The prayer Nehemiah offered at the beginning of the story is one of the most intense in Scripture, and he ended by reminding the Lord: "They are your servants and your people, whom you redeemed by your great strength and your mighty hand. Lord, let your ear be attentive to the prayer of this your servant and to the prayer of your servants who delight in revering your name" (Neh. 1:10–11).

Notice those words: ". . . whom you redeemed by your great strength." This referred to the Jewish repatriates who were now struggling to keep their nation alive, but it also refers in a broader sense to us. Through the blood of the Lord Jesus Christ, He has redeemed us by His great strength and mighty hand.

Nehemiah was deeply troubled. Those restored to the land by God's mighty strength now had little strength to advance their cause. Their walls were derelict. As the burden grew in Nehemiah's heart, a plan gelled in his mind. He knew deliverance could only come in the future as it had come in the past—by God's great strength. He felt God calling him to undertake a task so great it couldn't be accomplished by human means but only by divine force.

I wonder if you feel as I sometimes do. We're so overwhelmed with our responsibilities we forget the needs of a desperate world. The walls have been breached, and we're too busy to notice. But sometimes God taps us on the shoulder and says, "Do something about this." He gives us a challenge that can only be met by divine strength.

That's what happened to Bramwell Booth, the son of William Booth, who founded the Salvation Army. One day Bramwell entered his father's room and found him dressing and brushing his hair. The elder Booth didn't say "Good morning!" or engage in pleasantries. He looked at his son and cried, "Bramwell! Did you know that men slept out all night on the bridges?" William had arrived in London quite late the night before and had observed this during his ride home.

"Well, yes," said Bramwell, "a lot of poor fellows, I suppose."

"Then you ought to be ashamed of yourself to have known it and to have done nothing for them."

Bramwell began to explain the difficulties of adding a new humanitarian project to the work already being done, but William punctured the air with his hairbrush and shouted, "Go and do something!" That was the beginning of the Salvation Army Shelters, a special ministry that changed the lives of hundreds of homeless men during the early days of the Salvation Army work in London.[6]

"Go and do something" is what Christians have always done in the strength of the Lord. That's what we're called to do in a world of broken-down walls. Christianity has changed the planet more than any other philosophy or faith system ever conceived on our globe. Christians have been at the vanguard of the abolition of slavery, the promotion of human rights, the advance of prison reform, the establishing of child labor laws, the creation of hospitals and educational systems. We're the ones championing the rights of preborn children and the care of orphans and widows. At this very moment, armies of Christians are engaged all over the globe in feeding the hungry, providing clean drinking water, and granting relief in areas devastated by natural disasters. We're the ones taking the hope of the gospel to the downtrodden of the earth.

We can only do this because of God's great strength and His mighty hand.

Even if God doesn't call you to be a Nehemiah, a Booth, a Wilberforce, a Martin Luther, or a Martin Luther King Jr., He still wants to tap you on the shoulder and show you a need you can meet. He says to you and me: "Go and do something!" Somewhere near you there's a child to raise, a heart to heal, a parent to care for, a grandchild to love, a church to revitalize, a family to feed, a mission to support, a soul to save, a rift to mend, a note to send, a wall to build. We're to do it in His great strength.

OUR STRENGTH IS SMALL—NEHEMIAH 4:10

As his book unfolds, Nehemiah gained the blessing of the king and made the long and difficult journey to Jerusalem. After three days of rest, he mounted his horse for a moonlit tour around the destroyed walls of the city.

Earlier this year when I was in Jerusalem, I took a moonlit walk around the ramparts of the ancient walls of Jerusalem, but not the same ones Nehemiah built. The current wall around the Old City dates from the 1500s. Nonetheless, I could visualize Nehemiah's nocturnal tour as he surveyed the damage and formulated a plan in his mind. Once he knew what to do, he gathered the Jewish leaders and shared his vision for rebuilding the walls. With great excitement, they began. This was one of the best-organized building programs in history. Nehemiah 3 tells how one person after another tackled the section of the wall nearest his home. Nehemiah 4:6 says, "So we rebuilt the wall till all of it reached half its height, for the people worked with all their heart."

That's when the trouble began. Halfway through the project, local officials threatened the builders, and the opposition came close to shutting down the whole project. There was a danger of imminent attack. "But we prayed to our God and posted a guard day and night to meet this threat," says Nehemiah 4:9.

A wave of discouragement swept over the workers and infected the entire Jewish remnant. Nehemiah 4:10 says, "Meanwhile, the people in Judah said, 'The strength of the laborers is giving out, and there is so much rubble that we cannot rebuild the wall.'" That's the next occurrence of the word "strength" in the book of Nehemiah, and we can relate to it. How often our strength gives out halfway through a project. That's when most people give up—halfway through the project. *The strength of the laborers is giving out.* The task is harder than we anticipated, the resistance is greater, and there's much yet to do.

Some give up on their home halfway through their marriage. They give up on treatment halfway through rehab. They give up on their recovery. They give up on their diet, on their exercise program. They give up on a difficult child or resistant relative. They give up on their job before they've really persevered and done their best. They give up on the ministry God has given them. They give in to a stubborn temptation. They can't find the inner strength to keep improving, to keep praying, to keep growing, to keep loving, to persevere through the difficulty, to build up their work—whatever it is.

If we're doing something other than what God has ordained for us, maybe we *should* give up. But when God leads us to undertake His will for our lives, we only really begin when we come to the end of our own strength. He calls us to do things that can be started in our strength but must be completed in His.

Have you read any of the poems of Annie Johnson Flint? Her story illustrates this perfectly. Her mother died when she was very small, and she was taken in and raised by a woman whose husband had died in the Civil War. Annie became a schoolteacher, but early in her career she was disabled by severe arthritis and was told by doctors she'd soon be a helpless invalid. She moved into Clifton Springs Sanitarium and was confined to a wheelchair much like my wife, Katrina. Annie didn't know how to pay for her care, but with her painfully curled fingers she began writing poetry, word by word. When her strength gave out, she tapped into God's endless supply. She became a beloved poet whose words have endured, and I still find them enriching. One of her poems speaks of how easily our strength gives out in midstream, but how God's power is boundless.

> When we have exhausted our store of endurance,
> When our strength has failed ere the day is half done,
> When we reach the end of our hoarded resources,
> Our Father's full giving is only begun.
> His love has no limit; His grace has no measure.
> His power has no boundary known unto men;
> For out of His infinite riches in Jesus,
> He giveth, and giveth, and giveth again.[7]

How often we reach the end of our hoarded resources and our strength expires before the job is finished or the day is done. That's when we must learn to tap into God's electrical lines by the cable of prayer. Our Father transmits His boundless strength to us again and again. And that's what we see in the next occurrence of "strength" in Nehemiah.

WE PLEAD FOR GOD'S STRENGTH IN PRAYER—NEHEMIAH 6:9

The wall-builders in Nehemiah's day ran out of strength when the task was half-done, but their enemies seemed indefatigable. They sent a threatening challenge to Nehemiah, asking him to meet with them. His classic answer was "I am carrying on a great project and cannot go down. Why should the work stop while I leave it and go down to you?" (Neh. 6:3).

I've used this line twice in my ministry with two different men who sought to spook me. In both cases they wanted to draw me into a disagreement, hoping to glean some information to use against me. I quoted this verse to both of them, one face-to-face and the other in a letter. "I'm doing a great work," I said, "and cannot come down to talk with you."

My adversaries finally left me alone, but Nehemiah wasn't so lucky. Four more times, his opponents sent threatening messages. Nehemiah, however, wouldn't be drawn into the line of fire. Nehemiah 6:9 says, "They were all trying to frighten us, thinking, 'Their hands will get too weak for the work, and it will not be completed.' But I prayed. . . ."

What did Nehemiah pray?

But I prayed, "Now strengthen my hands." (Neh. 6:9)

That's the third occurrence of the word "strength" in the book of Nehemiah. Every day God gives us work to do and burdens to bear. His strength is great, but ours is small, and sometimes we're apt to give up before the work is completed or the burden is resolved. Our enemy seeks to discourage us, for he knows discouragement leads to defeat. He thinks our hands will get too weak for the work. But one simple, sincere prayer will save the day: "Now strengthen my hands." And somehow in God's timing you'll see the wall go up, the Devil back off, the Lord draw near, and the job followed through to the end.

Adopt that simple four-word prayer for yourself: "Now strengthen my hands." You'll find somehow the work will get gone. Nehemiah 6:15–16 says, "So the wall was completed in . . . fifty-two days. When all our enemies heard about this, all the surrounding nations were afraid and lost their self-confidence, because they realized that this work had been done with the help of our God."

Work done in the strength of the Lord is long-lasting, and I have archaeological proof of that. In 2007 the famed Jewish excavator Dr. Eilat Mazar discovered a portion of an ancient wall she dates to the days of Nehemiah. It's now unearthed and visible to those visiting the Old City of Jerusalem. Nehemiah's work has stood the test of time—and so will yours.

GOD IMPARTS HIS STRENGTH THROUGH JOY—NEHEMIAH 8:10

But there's one more verse about "strength" in Nehemiah, and it brings us to our primary text. If God's strength is great and ours is small and if we pray Nehemiah's prayer, asking for strength, how does the Lord answer? According to Nehemiah 8:10, He imparts His strength through joy, for the joy of the Lord is our strength.

Here's what happened. The city walls were finished at the end of Nehemiah 6, but the date for their dedication didn't occur until chapter 12. In the interval, the city officials announced a great open-air conference to study the Scriptures. In today's terms we'd say they decided to hold a Bible conference. Nehemiah 8:1 says, ". . . all the people came together as one in the square before the Water Gate." This must have been an expansive public plaza created by the new walls and gates. The text continues, "They told Ezra the teacher of the Law to bring out the Book of the Law of Moses, which the LORD had commanded for Israel."

A great crowd convened made up of men, women, and children—all who were old enough to understand. Standing on a high wooden platform with colleagues on his right and left, Ezra taught from the Law "from daybreak till noon as he faced the square before the Water Gate. . . . And all the people listened attentively" (verse 3). Verses 5–6 say, "All the people could see him because he was standing above them; and as he opened it, the people all stood up. Ezra praised the LORD, the great God; and all the people lifted their hands and responded, 'Amen! Amen!' Then they bowed down and worshipped the LORD with their faces to the ground."

Verse 8 is my favorite Bible verse about the craft of preaching. It's been my guide in preparing sermons for more than four decades: "So they read in the book in the law of God distinctly, and gave the sense, and caused them to understand the reading."[8] That, to me, is the essence of preaching and teaching. We read the Scriptures distinctly, give the sense or meaning, and show people how it applies to their lives. Ezra could do this because he was "well versed" in the Law, having devoted himself to studying the Scripture, obeying it, and teaching it to others (see Ezra 7:6 and 10).

The response was marvelous. As the people listened to what Ezra read in the Law—the commands of God and His promises—they began weeping. One person after another was overcome by a wave of grief. They'd been living in darkness so long they had organized their lives around it. They hadn't been observing the feasts and festivals comprising their heritage. They had neglected the Sabbath. They hadn't been faithful to the commands of God, nor had they taught their children about Yahweh. They had overlooked the blessings God offered them. They had disregarded His presence among them, and so much time had been lost. Soft sobs filled the air, then louder cries of regrets. Perhaps someone started wailing. A groundswell of emotion swept over the crowd that nearly careened out of control.

That's when Nehemiah stepped in to encourage the people to shift emotional gears. That's an important lesson to learn. Sometimes we feel we're powerless against the emotions coming over us, but we always have some level of control over our attitudes, especially when there's a spiritual basis to our lives. We have to tell ourselves: "I'm not going to let this emotion have free rein; I'm going to rein it in. I'm going to shift gears. I'm going to choose my reaction rather than being at the mercy of this tide of emotion rising within me. I'm going to adopt biblical attitudes in any and every circumstance."

Nehemiah told them to stop regretting the past and to start rejoicing in the present and in the future. He told them to start rejoicing in the Lord. "This day is holy to our Lord," he said. "Do not grieve, for the joy of the LORD is your strength" (Neh. 8:10).

The Levites fanned through the crowds, calming the people and saying, "Be still, for this is a holy day. Do not grieve" (Neh. 8:11). The crowd dispersed for lunch in high spirits, and "all the people went away to eat and drink . . . and to celebrate with great joy, because they now understood the words that had been made known to them" (v. 12).

The next day was the men's day at the Bible conference. All the men, considered the heads of households, gathered. As they continued studying the Law, they realized they had long neglected observing the Feast of Tabernacles. This was a fun-filled Jewish festival in which everyone in the country went camping in their backyards, in the public parks, and on their rooftops. It was to reenact the journey of the children of Israel from Egypt to the promised land, prompting them to remember they were still pilgrims and strangers on the earth. Since the actual dates of the Feast of Tabernacles were conveniently at hand, the nation went into overdrive preparing to celebrate. It would be like our realizing in mid-December to suddenly celebrate Christmas after years of neglect.

So the people went out and brought back branches and built themselves temporary shelters on their own roofs, in their courtyards, in the courts of the house of God, and in the square by the Water Gate and the one by the Gate of Ephraim. The whole company that had returned from exile built temporary shelters and lived in them. From the days of Joshua son of Nun until that day, the Israelites had not celebrated it like this. And their joy was very great. (Neh. 8:16–17)

Day by day, the Bible conference continued as Ezra read from the book of the Law; the people rejoiced, and the children relished camping with their parents on the rooftops and public squares of Jerusalem. The surge of revival and joy they experienced that week gave them strength for days and years to come. In studying the great revivals of Christian history, I've often noticed how a surge of revival will propel the Lord's work to the next generation. The Jesus Movement of the 1970s, for example, cannonballed an entire generation of young people (including me) into the Lord's work with an enthusiasm that has lasted for decades. In Nehemiah 8, the Water Gate revival galvanized the Jewish people to strengthen their nation and keep the messianic hope alive. It paved the way for the eventual coming of the Messiah.

This, then, is the pattern we find. God's strength is very great, and He calls us to join Him in fulfilling His will on earth. We do our best, but often, about halfway through, our strength gives out. We grow discouraged, and sometimes we're on the verge of giving up. But when we cry out to God for strength, He gives us His Word. He gives us His promise. He gives it to us distinctly, helping us make sense of it and enabling us to understand how it applies to our lives. That brings a surge of joy, which imparts the strength needed to bear the burdens, fulfill the work, and finish the job. It's as though the Lord installs an efficient little high-voltage generator within us—the word *joy* embossed on its side—that lights up our faces and gives us the energy needed to do whatever He asks. He moves us from regretting the past to rejoicing in the present. He helps us put things behind us, face the future with courage, and rejoice in His grace.

There's something about the joy of the Lord that transmits strength to us as if we were connected to a divine generator, as if we were connected to Jesus Himself. Learning, memorizing, praying, and practicing Nehemiah 8:10 is like investing in the 810 Power Company. It sends energy into our bones. It lights up our eyes and gives a glow to our faces. It keeps us from organizing our lives around the darkness.

I once asked my friend Cliff Barrows, who led the great stadium crusades for Billy Graham, if, during all his years of ministry, he ever grew discouraged or encountered bouts of depression. He thought a moment before saying something I found hard to believe. "Robert," he told me, "I have never known a despondent day."

"How can you say that?" I asked. "I've had plenty of despondent days."

"Because," he said with characteristic enthusiasm in every word, "the joy of the Lord is the strength of my life."

Perhaps we can't avoid an occasional despondent day, but we'll have fewer and fewer of them when we learn to invest in God's power company and generate the energy of His strength from turbines of joy.

A WORD FROM KATRINA

I began the habit of morning devotions as a young adult in Florida. Later, as a young mother, I would tell my children to go to their rooms and play quietly while I had my quiet time. After awhile, they discovered they enjoyed doing that. I tried to never miss my morning time with the Lord, for daily Bible study changed me, just like Romans 12:2 says—we are transformed by the renewing of our minds. Something about that process translated into literal physical strength for me. I believe that's what Nehemiah meant when he said "The joy of the LORD is your strength."

I'm thankful I had this habit firmly in place before I became disabled. Now more than ever, I depend on my morning times of Bible study and prayer to keep a joyful and strong frame of mind. Whatever our circumstances, God will give us joy when we spend personal time with Him in His Word and prayer. Somehow it even gives us physical strength for each day. It helps us go on, whatever our situation.

FOUR

Occupy a Fortress

God is our refuge and strength.

PSALM 46:1

"Victoria and the girls have been in a wreck," my son-in-law, Ethan, told me over the phone. He said their van had veered off the road, slid down a hill, burst through a fence, and slammed against a tree. One of the kids found a cell phone on the floorboard and called him, saying, "We've had a wreck and Mommy's asleep." Paramedics were on the way, and so was Ethan, who suggested I head to the hospital.

It's hard to describe the fear one feels in such moments. I struggled to stay calm enough to think, to tell Katrina, to find my keys and billfold and to pull out of the driveway. But just as the worst scenarios were stampeding through my mind, a passage of Scripture came to me. It was a chapter I'd been re-memorizing—Psalm 46: "God is our refuge and strength, a very present help in trouble. Therefore we will not fear. . . ."[1]

Those words became my lifeline, and by the time I got to the hospital I was functional again—still frightened and upset, but able to respond to the situation. I identified myself to paramedics who were exiting the building and asked, "How are they?"

"They'll be all right," came the welcome answer.

My heart was still pounding like a sledgehammer as I visited one after another in their emergency cubicles, and it took a long time for us all to calm down. I hope to never again encounter such fear; but, of course, we can't always avoid uninvited trauma. Events come unwelcomed and unexpected. But on that day, I was grateful for Psalm 46 and the strength it gave me as it rang inside my heart.

Words as robust as those of Psalm 46 don't flow from ordinary events. Something dramatic must have prompted the man who composed them. Many Bible scholars believe this psalm was written against the backdrop of the Assyrian invasion of Judah about seven hundred years before Christ. In those days, a godly king named Hezekiah sat on the throne of Judah, and the prophet Isaiah preached regularly in Jerusalem. A sense of revival was in the air, but also a growing sense of foreboding. Rumors were reaching Jerusalem of a vast empire to the east, marching slowly but inexorably toward them—the invincible forces of King Sennacherib of Assyria. These invading legions represented the greatest military machine the world had seen—and the cruelest. Events were closing in. War seemed unavoidable, defeat inevitable, and everyone knew the Assyrians were merciless toward their victims.

When they reached the borders of Israel, the Assyrians swarmed in like locusts. The Northern Kingdom quickly collapsed and was destroyed forever. The Southern Kingdom of Judah was breached, the forward cities fell, the defensive perimeters crumbled, and the nation was occupied. Only Jerusalem remained, its residents trapped. According to the Bible, the city was surrounded like a hut in a cucumber field. Isaiah described the armies of Assyria as a flood that swirled over the land, passed through it, and reached up to its neck (see Isa. 1:8 and 8:8). Sennacherib had his own metaphor. He had trapped Hezekiah, he said, like a caged bird.[2]

With victory imminent, Sennacherib sent an envoy to Hezekiah with terms of surrender. But Hezekiah wasn't about to capitulate. In one of the most poignant scenes of prayer in the Bible, he took Sennacherib's letter to the temple, spread it before the Lord, and beseeched God for help, saying, "It is true, LORD, that the Assyrian kings have laid waste these nations and their lands. They have thrown their gods into the fire and destroyed them, for they were not gods but only wood and stone, fashioned by human hands. Now, LORD our God, deliver us from his hand, so that all the kingdoms of the earth may know that you alone, LORD, are God" (2 Kings 19:17–19).

That's the night God turned history on its head. That evening a lone angelic warrior descended from the ramparts of heaven and destroyed the Assyrian army. In one night, 185,000 enemy troops mysteriously perished without a shot being fired. Secular historians cannot explain it. When I was last in London, I visited the exhibitions in the British Museum related to Assyria and King Sennacherib, including the Taylor Prism, in which Sennacherib later wrote of this event. He never explained why he didn't take Jerusalem, capture its king, or defeat the nation of Judah. It's a remarkable fact of ancient history that the steamrolling Assyrians somehow failed to capture Jerusalem or to make tiny Judah a province of mighty Assyria. The Jewish nation never became part of the Assyrian Empire, which may explain why Sennacherib was later assassinated in his own house by his own sons.

Many scholars believe Psalm 46 was written to commemorate Judah's deliverance, and that would explain its intrepid tone. That also explains why it's so powerful for us. If God could save Hezekiah and his city from annihilation, He can surely help you and me in the distresses and distractions of life. If a single angel could rescue a nation, think of how the Lord and His angelic hosts can strengthen you. God is our refuge and strength, a very present help in trouble.

You'll gain strength from Psalm 46 even if you only know its opening verse, but the whole psalm is short enough to memorize and well worth the effort. When we look at all eleven verses, we have a threefold picture of the God who is our Refuge, our River, and our Ruler—and who shows us how to stand up to our own Sennacheribs.

OUR REFUGE

The verse begins by saying, "God is our refuge." When we talk about places of refuge today, we think of panic rooms, safe places, and super bunkers. In recent years, an extensive construction project has taken place beneath the West Wing of the White House. It's believed a new super bunker is being constructed, one able to survive any doomsday attack on our country, whether nuclear, biological, chemical, cyber, or radiological. At the same time, there are rumors of super bunkers under construction in Moscow, capable of holding large numbers of people. Imagine a place where you could be absolutely and utterly and completely safe no matter what happened.

There is no place of ultimate safety on earth, and there never will be. But we do have such a place in Christ. He's our hiding place, our refuge, our shelter of safety. The word "refuge" is used many times in the book of Psalms to describe our Lord in this way. I looked up every occurrence, and I found something interesting. The term "refuge" is used over and over, but the image associated with it changes from one passage to the next. It's as though the Lord wants us to understand this word in all its dimensions. He gives us several portraits to ponder and visualize.

First, God is our refuge like a rock. Psalm 18:2 says, "My God is my rock, in whom I take refuge." The writer of Psalm 71 prayed, "Be my rock of refuge, to which I can always go" (v. 3). Many of the psalms were written by David, who often hid from pursuing armies by disappearing into the network of caves that honeycombed the Judean hills. His life was often in danger, but God provided a system of built-in bunkers that kept him as safe as any modern bomb shelter. To David, this was a symbol of a great reality.

God is our rock. He is our cave. He is the one of whom we sing: "Rock of Ages, cleft for me; let me hide myself in Thee."³ Close your eyes and imagine finding absolute safety from storms and foes within a rocky cleft.

Second, God is our refuge like a shield. Psalm 18:30 says, "The LORD's word is flawless; he shields all who take refuge in him." Psalm 119:114 adds, "You are my refuge and my shield; I have put my hope in your word." In biblical times, warriors positioned themselves behind their shields to deflect the blows of the enemy just as police officers and soldiers today use body armor and riot shields. The psalmist was saying, "God is my wraparound shield. He protects me on every side." Visualize that whenever your insecurities flair up.

Third, God is our refuge like a tower. Psalm 61:3 says, "For you have been my refuge, a strong tower against the foe." In biblical times towers afforded a sense of security by providing thick walls and high elevations. From the top of a tower, a warrior had gravity on his side. The arrows aimed toward him slowed as they flew upward, but the weapons he employed from atop the tower rained down destruction on the foes.

As our tower, the Lord gives us preservation and elevation. He Himself is between our enemies and us, and through Him we rise above our circumstances. The Bible says, "The name of the LORD is a fortified tower; the righteous run to it and are safe" (Prov. 18:10). Can you conceptualize running into a tower, bolting the door, and ascending the steps? Just today I received a letter from a friend who told me he's no longer going to use the phrase "under the circumstances" to describe his life. We serve a God who is always above the circumstances, he said, and should view things from the heights of heaven.

Fourth, God is our refuge like a shelter. Psalm 31:19–20 says, "How abundant are the good things that you have stored up for those . . . who take refuge in you. In the shelter of your presence you hide them from all human intrigues; you keep them safe in your dwelling from accusing tongues."

Many of our problems come from the words of others. It's terrible when someone criticizes you with hurtful words. Much of my counseling has been to people who've been hurt by what someone said to them—often a parent or close family member.

If you've ever been caught in the rain, you know what it's like to look for a canopy, a storefront, a hut, a house, or even a friend with an umbrella. There you found a refuge and a shelter. Perhaps you're encountering stormy weather today. Has someone upset you? Argued with you? Treated you rudely? People are always trying to rain on our parades, but when it rains it's best to seek shelter. He Himself is our shelter from human intrigues and accusing tongues.

Fifth, God is our refuge like wings. In Psalm 57:1, David wrote, "I take refuge in the shadow of your wings until the disaster has passed." Psalm 91 says, "He will cover you with his feathers, and under his wings you will find refuge" (v. 4).

I recall visiting my grandparents on their farm in North Carolina, watching the baby chicks disappear beneath their mother when I got too close. I couldn't figure out how so many babies could crowd under one fat old hen, but she knew how to ruffle her feathers and take them all in. Recently I saw a remarkable picture of a swan floating across the lake with six fuzzy babies tucked neatly aboard her back and covered by her ample wing. For those chicks and goslings, there's no more secure spot on earth.

Christians in Soviet days, when threatened by Communist officials, reminded themselves that the iron curtain and bamboo curtain were no match for God's feather curtain. It's an unusual but accurate way of visualizing God's care for us. Jesus used this analogy by comparing Himself to a hen wanting to gather her chicks under her wings (Matt. 23:37). It reminds me of the old hymn "Under His wings I am safety abiding, though the night deepens and tempests are wild."[4]

Sixth, God is our refuge like a fortress. Psalm 59:16 says, "You are my fortress, my refuge in times of trouble." Psalm 91:2 says, "He is my refuge and my fortress, my God, in whom I trust." That's the way the writer of Psalm

46 thought of God, and some translations render this term in Psalm 46 as "fortress." Our God is a castle, a citadel around us. That, too, is an image worth visualizing. If you're afraid or worried right now, if you feel weak and helpless, just close your eyes and meditate on the towering, shielding, protecting walls of God's presence around your life. See yourself inside a fortress beyond the reach of any foe.

In 1527, Martin Luther fell into a deep depression after learning his friend Leonhard Kaiser had been burned at the stake in the Netherlands for holding to Reformation doctrines. Luther felt guilty, for he was at home in his own safe bed while his associates were imprisoned and facing execution. But Luther turned to Psalm 46 and pondered it so vividly he was able to paint a picture in song, giving us one of the greatest hymns in Christian history based on Psalm 46: "Ein feste Burg ist unser Gott."[5]

> A mighty fortress is our God, a bulwark never failing;
> Our helper He, amid the flood of mortal ills prevailing.

We have all these visualizations, but in practical terms what does it mean? These pictures provide mental ammunition against the fears of life. We never know what's going to happen next. We don't know what's going to happen to us, to those we love, to our nation, or to our world. But our foes and fears cannot withstand our true, biblical faith. No alarm is higher than His power, deeper than His love, or more potent than His promises. We can run to Him and hide ourselves in Him, and we can always say God is my rock, my shield, my fortress, my tower, my dwelling place, and under His wings I find refuge.

When my friend David Jeremiah was in his fifties and at the prime of his ministry, his doctor discovered a mass in his abdomen. The diagnosis came back, and it was cancer. Dr. Jeremiah battled the disease and by the grace of God overcame it. But the worst was yet to come, for he was diagnosed a second time. He later wrote: "My cancer was back, with a vengeance, and that was nearly impossible for me to accept. I had celebrated a victory over the dread disease. I had put it behind me, assigning it to the closed files of my unhappy memories. I had determined to live happily ever after. But the road had come to another bend—if anything, an even crueler one. It felt almost like mockery to my sense of gratitude to God for bringing me through it before. My mood went black. Could I survive another weary bout with the giant? It was the darkest night of my soul . . . ."

But he found refuge in Psalm 46. As Dr. Jeremiah meditated on the words "God is my refuge," he said he realized God is an *awesome* refuge. He is an *accessible* refuge. And He is an *ageless* refuge. "When trouble comes, we can retreat to our refuge, who is awesome, available, and ageless. No problem is any match for Him."[6]

Whether we live or die, the eternal God is our refuge, and our real safety is in Him through Christ. The Bible says, "Since, then, you have been raised with Christ, set your hearts on things above . . . for you died, and your life is now hidden with Christ in God" (Col. 3:1–3).

But the verse doesn't stop after the first four words. It goes on to say: "God is our refuge *and strength*." This is the external/internal provision of the Lord. A refuge is something outside you. Suppose the enemy is chasing you, but you see a friendly castle nearby. Running as hard as you can, you outrun the pursuer and race across the moat as the drawbridge lifts behind you. As the gate clanks shut, you are safely shielded and enclosed, free from further alarm. The fortress is all around you. The walls are before and behind you. The pavement is beneath you. The ramparts and bulwarks are above you. You are inside the fortress, and the fortress is outside of you, surrounding you and separating you from your pursuers.

But strength is something that's inside of you. It's an internal word. According to Psalm 46:1, the same God who is our *refuge on the outside* is our *strength on the inside.*

Furthermore, He's *our help on the downside* of life. Notice what comes next: "God is our refuge and strength, a very present help in trouble."[7] See how this sentence telescopes out to us.

- God is a help.
- He is a *present* help.
- He is a *very* present help.
- He is a very present help *in trouble*.

The word "help" occurs in the Bible more than 250 times. The Bible says He descends from heaven to help us (Deut. 33:26–27). He helps us when we are overwhelmed (2 Chron. 14:11). He helps us as we look up to Him (Ps. 121). He helps us when we pray (Heb. 4:16). He helps us as we trust Him (Ps. 28:7). He provides the help of the Holy Spirit, who lives within us, and He is able to help us in temptation (2 Tim. 1:14; Heb. 2:18). He will never leave us or forsake us, so we may say with confidence, "The Lord is my helper; I will not be afraid" (Heb. 13:6).

The first stanza of Psalm 46 tells us God is our refuge and strength, a very present help in trouble, so we needn't be afraid even if the earth gives way and the mountains fall into the seas.

OUR RIVER

The middle stanza of Psalm 46 talks about a river: "There is a river whose streams make glad the city of God, the holy place where the Most High dwells" (v. 4). The charm of many of the great cities of the world is in their rivers. In London, it's the Thames. In Paris, the Seine. In Vienna, the Danube. In Cairo, the Nile. In Washington, the Potomac. Nearly every great city has a great river.

But one ancient capital has no river, lake, or body of water—Jerusalem. It's as dry as dust. Yet in Psalm 46 we have this intriguing verse: "There is a river, the streams whereof shall make glad the city of God, the holy place of the tabernacles of the most High" (v. 4, KJV). What was the writer talking about?

A couple of possibilities present themselves. The writer could have been referring to the New Jerusalem, the Holy City of Heaven, which has a river flowing from the throne of God (see Rev. 22:1). But there's another option. As I said, most scholars believe Psalm 46 was an Israeli national psalm composed to commemorate the deliverance of Judah during the Assyrian invasion. When Hezekiah realized his capital would be surrounded by the greatest military force in the world, he shored up its defenses. In 2 Chronicles 32:2–3, 30, we read: "When Hezekiah saw that Sennacherib had come and that he intended to wage war against Jerusalem, he consulted with his officials and military staff about blocking off the water from the springs outside the city, and they helped him. . . . It was Hezekiah who blocked the upper outlet of the Gihon spring and channeled the water down to the west side of the City of David."

Second Kings 20:20 adds, "As for the other events in Hezekiah's reign, all his achievements and how he made the pool and the tunnel by which he brought water into the city, are they not written in the book of the annals of the kings of Judah?"

This is referring to one of the most famous archaeological discoveries in old Jerusalem—Hezekiah's tunnel. In biblical times Jerusalem had only one primary source of water: the Gihon Spring on the eastern side of the city at the bottom of the hill in the vicinity of the Kidron Valley. It's one of the world's major intermittent springs, and it provided abundant water for the city. The early residents of Jerusalem built the Pool of Siloam as a reservoir to hold the waters, but this was at the bottom of the hill outside the walls of the ancient city.

Hezekiah proposed digging a long, narrow tunnel under the streets of Jerusalem to divert the water from the Pool of Siloam to an unground repository beneath the city, and to sink a shaft or well to the cistern so the Assyrians would find no water outside the walls while giving Jerusalem its own underground river within the walls.

According to an ancient inscription (now in a museum in Istanbul), workers began working on both extremities—one group at the Gihon Spring tunneling inward, and the other group at the bottom of the shaft tunneling outward. Somehow they met in the middle. Why did they do it this way? In those days it would have been hard to meet in the middle, and, indeed, the tunnel zigzags.

But time was of the essence. The invasion was near, and one city after another was falling to the Assyrians. Jewish engineers doubled the speed of the project by working at both ends toward the middle. Somehow they met, and a channel was opened to bring water into an underground repository under the city streets. Hezekiah's Tunnel is 1,750 feet long and considered one of the greatest works of water engineering technology in antiquity. It was lost to history until 1838, when an archaeologist named Edward Robinson rediscovered it.

I've had the privilege of wading through Hezekiah's Tunnel on several occasions, but the first was the most memorable. It was before the tunnel was opened to the public. A friend and I hiked down the Kidron Valley into the Arab village of Silwan where we found an Arab fellow and offered him money if he could figure out how to get us into Hezekiah's Tunnel. He disappeared a few moments, then came back with a key and some candles and flip-flops. There was an iron door into the mountain and an old padlock. The fellow unlocked the door, and it creaked open. The inside was black as night. He told us to strip off our pants, and we sloshed into the watery cave, wading by candlelight with water reaching our waists. I can truly say it was one of the most unique experiences of my life.

If Psalm 46 was a national celebration over God's deliverance from Sennacherib, this verse makes sense historically. While not technically a river, this underground current helped save Israel and lifted the morale of the Jerusalemites. Many commentators believe this is what the psalmist was referring to. God enabled them to find a source of water to save their city, an underground stream that made glad the city of God.

Think of it. On the surface, there was no water. No river. No refreshment. No life-giving currents. Outside the city, an amassed army. But deep below the level of the streets and homes, beneath the ground level of ancient Jerusalem, there was a hidden river coursing through the rocks. There was a secret spring, a reliable source of water to refresh the trapped inhabitants who, though besieged, were assured of victory. Thus said the psalmist, "There is a river whose streams make glad the city of God."

There's spiritual meaning here. Far beneath the ground level of life, below our homes and streets and everyday activities, there is a secret spring for Christians—a reliable source of refreshment the enemy cannot figure out, and whose flow cannot be interrupted.

The greatest underground current in the universe is the river of the Holy Spirit flowing beneath the surface of our lives and available to keep us hydrated and refreshed while we're under siege in this life and awaiting the victory assured us in Christ. Psalm 87:7 says, "All my springs are in you." He keeps us alive and rejuvenated even when encircled by our enemy.

How do we sink our buckets into this river?

First, recognize only Jesus can meet our critical inner needs. In the story of the Samaritan woman in John 4, Jesus sat by a well and spoke to this lonely woman, telling her, "Whoever drinks the water I give them will never thirst. Indeed, the water I give them will become in them a spring of water welling up to eternal life" (v. 14). As she came to know Him, her frustrations fell away as she found all her emotional needs met by the relationship she established with Christ. He quenched the thirst of her heart.

He can do the same for you. Jonathan Edwards wrote of Christ's infinite flow of grace, saying, "A thirsty man does not sensibly lessen a river by quenching his thirst. Christ is like a river. . . . A river is continually flowing, there are fresh supplies of water coming from the fountainhead continually, so that a man may live by it, and be supplied with water all his life. So Christ is an ever-flowing fountain; He is continually supplying His people and the fountain is not spent."[8]

In the book of Jeremiah, the Lord lamented, "My people are guilty of two evils: They have abandoned me, the spring of living waters; and instead, they have settled for dead and stagnant water from cracked, leaky cisterns of their own making" (Jer. 2:13).[9]

Start, then, with Christ.

Second, we can pray every day for the fullness of the Holy Spirit. In John 7, we read: "On the last and greatest day of the Feast, Jesus stood and said in a loud voice, 'If anyone is thirsty, let him come to me and drink. Whoever believes in Me, as the Scripture has said, streams of living water will flow from within him.' By this He meant the Spirit, whom those who believed in Him were later to receive" (vv. 37–39).

It's the Holy Spirit who pours the resources of Christ into our lives. The Bible says, "God's love has been poured out into our hearts through the Holy Spirit, who has been given to us" (Rom. 5:5). It's a good idea to rededicate yourself to the Lord Jesus every morning and ask Him to fill you with His Spirit.

Third, we draw from our underground river when we study God's Word and meditate on it. Psalm 1 says, "Blessed is the one . . . whose delight is in the law of the LORD, and who meditates on his law day and night. That person is like a tree planted by streams of water, which yields its fruit in season and whose leaf does not wither—whatever they do prospers" (vv. 1–3).

Fourth, as we meditate on God's Word, we can claim His promises by faith and trust Him completely. Jeremiah 17:7–8 says, "Blessed is the one who trusts in the LORD, whose confidence is in him. He will be like a tree planted by the water that sends out its roots by the stream. It does not fear when heat comes; its leaves are always green. It has no worries in a year of drought and never fails to bear fruit."

Just as a tree gains strength from the channels of water at its roots, so we're strengthened by Him who is our refuge and our river—and our ruler.

OUR RULER

The last stanza of Psalm 46 reminds us of God's sovereign rule: "Come, behold the works of the LORD, who has made desolations in the earth. He makes wars cease to the end of the earth; He breaks the bow and cuts the spear in two; He burns the chariot in the fire. Be still, and know that I am God; I will be exalted among the nations, I will be exalted in the earth! The LORD of hosts is with us; the God of Jacob is our refuge."[10]

Imagine writing this after seeing how God delivered your city from 185,000 encircling soldiers.

Never forget who holds controlling interest in this world. Whatever happens, the Lord is in charge, both of the universe and of you. Whatever the circumstances, His throne is limitless in power and eternal in duration. The armies of Sennacherib are no match for Him who breaks the bow, shatters the spear, and burns the chariots with fire. No adversary can threaten Him. No foe can fell Him. He reigns supreme, unequalled, unrivaled, undaunted. Before Him every knee will bow.

And *this* Lord Almighty is with us; *this* God of Jacob is our refuge. So be still and remember He is God. Calm down. Relax. Rely. Rejoice. There's no need to panic. He's the Creator and Sustainer of the universe, and He will take care of the things that concern you.

This is the same advice God gave Israel at the Red Sea in Exodus 14:13–14: "Do not be afraid. Stand firm and you will see the deliverance the LORD will bring you today. . . . The LORD will fight for you. You need only to be still."

This is the advice God gave King Jehoshaphat in 2 Chronicles 20:15–17: "Do not be afraid or discouraged because of this vast army. For the battle is not yours, but God's. . . . You will not have to fight this battle. Take up your positions; stand firm and see the deliverance the LORD will give you. . . . Do not be afraid; do not be discouraged . . . the LORD will be with you."

This is the same advice Jesus gave the apostles in John 14:1: "Do not let your hearts be troubled. You believe in God, believe also in Me."

You can take whatever situation you're facing and give it the Psalm 46:10 treatment: Be still, calm down, pull yourself together, remember God is in control even when the ground shifts beneath your feet and the mountains tumble into the sea.

Psalm 46 been called the Earthquake Psalm because it avows God is an unchanging refuge in tectonic times. Perhaps it also acquired that title because of a series of events that shook London in 1750. On February 8, an earthquake rattled the British capital. It rumbled and radiated from the southeast region of London and terrified the whole city. Not only did the buildings shake, but there were reverberating noises like thunder enveloping the scene. Inhabitants, struck with fear, ran into the streets, afraid of being buried alive in their swaying homes.

A month later, evangelist Charles Wesley was beginning an early morning sermon when another earthquake—a far worse one—struck. Worshippers panicked, fearing their church building, the Foundry, would collapse. People screamed. Children cried. Wesley had the presence of mind to quote Psalm 46 with its dramatic imagery: "We will not fear though the earth be removed, and the hills be carried into the midst of the sea . . . for the LORD of hosts is with us; the God of Jacob is our refuge" (vv. 2, 7). He later said God filled his heart with faith and his mouth with words to calm and comfort the listeners.

Ten days later another earthquake rattled the south coast of England, and a prognosticator predicted an even greater one in the near future. His words were widely accepted and people lived in fear. They camped out in the streets and squares afraid their houses would fall. Multitudes turned to the Lord, thinking the Day of Judgment was near.

That final predicted earthquake never came, but to reassure the populace, Wesley published two small collections of hymns that have since been referred to as his "Earthquake Hymns." One of them is based on Psalm 46.

God, the omnipresent God,
Our strength and refuge stands
Ready to support our load,
And bear us in His hands.[11]

A lot of things can shake our lives. This planet isn't a secure place; but our immutable God—our Jesus, who is the same yesterday, today, and forever—provides refuge on the outside, strength on the inside, and help on the downside of life. He is our refuge, our river, our ruler.

Sherry Anderson, who has served as my assistant many years, told me that early in her marriage she and her husband, Michael, were watching a documentary painting the future in bleak colors. "I was young and a new Christian with a little baby," she said. "The thought of a troubling future was disturbing to me. I couldn't sleep that night and I worked myself into a panic. I couldn't calm down and kept replaying what I'd seen on TV over and over. Suddenly I heard the words of Psalm 46:10. They were so real they seemed to be audible: 'Be still and know that I am God.'

"I woke up Michael and asked him if he had quoted those words to calm me down, but he assured me he hadn't said a word. But I took the words to heart and knew God had spoken them to me. I calmed down, thanked Him for His protection and preeminence over sin, and fell peacefully asleep on the strength of that promise. Now when I hear or read things in the news that are disturbing, that verse always comes to mind and I can smile, remembering He is absolutely in control."[12]

While working on this chapter, I've been re-memorizing Psalm 46 so I can always quote it word for word at a moment's notice. Why don't you do the same?

God is our refuge and our strength,
Our ever present aid,
And, therefore, though the earth remove,
We will not be afraid.[13]

A WORD FROM KATRINA

Emergencies can be large or small, and they may occur at home or abroad. Several years ago, Robert and I used our frequent flyer miles to go to Paris for our anniversary. A travel agent specializing in disability helped us, and all went well—except for one tense episode.

We were told the easiest way from the airport to our hotel would be the train, but when we arrived in the underground Paris station, the elevator wasn't working. "You should have called first," the attendant said. "You'll have to go back to the airport."

Well, that didn't go over very well. When no one started the elevator, Rob decided to carry me up the stairs. The attendant said it wasn't allowed; but Rob said, "Well, I am going to carry my wife up those steps, and I could use your help." To his credit, the young man dutifully followed, grabbed our luggage and wheelchair, and scurried up the steps behind us. How we made it up those steps, I'm not sure; but when we emerged to street level, there was our hotel. From that point, we had a wonderful time in the City of Light.

In every disruption, daily frustration, and uncomfortable emergency, God is our strength and very present help. He keeps us going. He never leaves us; He's never busy, never on a break, never loses interest or is tired.

When life's elevators fail, He lifts us up.

FIVE

Stand Sequoia-Like
Above the Noise

In quietness and trust is your strength.

ISAIAH 30:15

Elena Chevalier is a journalist—the former copy editor of a New England newspaper—and a pastor's wife in the White Mountains of New Hampshire. She recently told me something that happened twenty years ago during a period of stubborn discouragement.

"I remember sunlight glistened off the soap bubbles as I filled the kitchen sink that Tuesday morning," she said. "It was a glorious day outside, but my heart couldn't relate. I scrubbed the dirty breakfast dishes and rinsed them mechanically. Tears spilled down my cheeks blurring my sight.

"For nearly two decades my husband and I had served in a large, prosperous New England church. Then a series of unfortunate events caused Wayne to resign his position as associate pastor and principal of the school our three children attended. His pastor wanted him to reconsider his resignation and stay, but we knew the differences were irreconcilable."

The aftereffects of that decision lingered. Elena's heart was invested in her husband's calling, but now they felt like wanderers in the wilderness. That morning as Elena prayed over the dirty dishes, the Lord drew near. "With a sun-sparkled, soapy hand on the faucet—I can still see it now—I sensed the Father's still, small voice speaking to me, reassuring me our lives were in His hands. If He wanted, He could easily cause someone to contact us even that very day."

That's just what happened.

"The letter arrived in the mail that afternoon. Goosebumps rose on my skin as my husband and I read the letter from a friend offering him a position as principal of a newly reopened school. The timing seemed so incredible. And yet, there were important concerns causing us to hesitate. Was this truly God's perfect will for us? We decided to pray and wait on God for absolute assurance.

"I went to the Scriptures as I always do, and there I found my answer in Isaiah 30:15. 'For thus saith the LORD GOD, the Holy One of Israel; In returning and rest shall ye be saved; in quietness and in confidence shall be your strength . . .'"[1]

Elena highlighted that verse in her heavily marked Bible, and in the margin she wrote: "Major life-changing decision to move and resume full-time Christian service. Within our hearts is peace that passes understanding: quietness and confidence in our Father in heaven, and in our own hearts."

That was two decades ago, and the Bible Elena used now resides in a retirement home for old Bibles in her bookcase, replaced by a newer one. But as she reviewed the story for me, she retrieved the older Bible and turned to Isaiah 30:15. She said, "Seeing the verse highlighted in restful aqua blue in that Bible instantly brought me back to that sun glinting off the soap suds in my sink and the time our Father taught me to return my worried thoughts to Him and to rest in Him."[2]

In quietness and confidence shall be your strength.

Eight words. Two qualities. One result. What a great formula for decoding the events in life! That phrase says it all: In quietness and confidence shall be your strength. When we're loud and rattled, we're weak—which says something about the state of the world right now. An empty box rattles, and an unlatched gate beats against the post. But a silent river runs deep, and a quiet and confident person stands out like a giant sequoia among the pines.

The quiet confidence of Isaiah 30:15 can carry us through many hardships, but how did that verse come to be in the Bible in the first place? When I read a verse so lovely, I want to know its context and background. What was on the prophet's mind when he wrote that phrase? In keeping with my approach in this book, I want to look at the tale behind the text. What caused Isaiah to compose these words?

The background of Isaiah 30 is similar to that of Psalm 46, but written before the Assyrian invasion, not afterward. The Assyrian army was the greatest force the world had ever seen. It rumbled over the world like a steamroller and seemed unstoppable. There were wars and conflicts everywhere, with Judah caught in the middle. On their southwestern flank the Egyptian empire was threatening. To the northeast, Sennacherib cast his cruel gaze toward them.

But Sennacherib didn't realize how dangerous it was to attack the people of God. Based on God's covenants with Abraham and David, Judah was the world's one and only true theocracy—a place where the God of eternity lived and ruled and reigned among His people through kings in the Davidic line. Jerusalem was the home of the temple, where God's presence literally dwelled in the form of the shekinah glory. This was the land of the Law of God and of the prophets. Here lived the Abrahamic chain of descendancy through which the Messiah was coming into the world. This was a nation with a special covenant with God, exceptional blessings, a unique place and purpose in history. The Lord had promised to preserve and protect Israel. He had sworn to bless those who blessed Israel and curse those who cursed Israel, so long as Israel remained faithful to Him.

Yahweh had sworn Himself as their supernatural ally. In times of conflict and danger, the kings and the people of Judah were commanded to turn to the Lord and trust Him, for they were under His safekeeping. Their national cry of victory was "The battle is the Lord's." Over and again, the Israelites had been delivered by Jehovah's mighty hand.

The same is true for God's children today—for those who know and love Jesus Christ. We're under the blessings of the new covenant, and Romans 8 declares, "If God is for us, who can be against us? . . . in all these things we are more than conquerors through him who loved us" (vv. 31, 37). The Bible says, "Thanks be to God! He gives us the victory through our Lord Jesus Christ" (1 Cor. 15:57). The apostle John said, "This is the victory that has overcome the world, even our faith" (1 John 5:4). As God's children, every problem or peril becomes an opportunity for God to work all things for our good. That's the basis for our supernatural optimism, which the Bible calls "hope."

In the Old Testament, these assurances undergirded the Hebrews. Among all the nations of the world, Judah was in a category all by itself in that no additional strategic alliances were needed or wanted. In fact, to run to a pagan nation seeking a military pact to ward off an enemy was an admission God's promises could not be trusted.

Yet during the invasion of Sennacherib, that's what happened. The king of Judah—Isaiah didn't identify which one—worried about the growing Assyrian threat, sent a delegation down to Egypt to broker some kind of mutual defense pact without even consulting the Lord as to what to do. They acted like virtual atheists, as though God were not a part of the equation of their situation at all. They failed to rely on their Redeemer.

Isaiah 30 is the sermon Isaiah preached when this diplomatic mission left for Egypt. It had apparently been a public event, a colorful spectacle, much talked about. A caravan made up of donkeys, diplomats, camels, and cash departed through one of the ancient gates. The envoys aired their noses in the direction of Egypt, hoping to secure military help in the face of the growing Assyrian threat.

Isaiah probably watched the convoy leave the city, and he had something to say about it. The sermon he preached on that day is recorded in chapter 30. He was a powerful preacher, an eloquent orator, and an articulate writer, and he framed his argument in words designed to capture the attention and imagination of his listeners.

The opening word of his sermon in Isaiah 30:1 tells us how he felt about the mission: "Woe . . ."

Woe to the obstinate children, declares the Lord, to those who carry out plans that are not mine, forming an alliance, but not by my Spirit, heaping sin upon sin; who go down to Egypt without consulting me; who look for help to Pharaoh's protection . . . (vv. 1–2)

Isaiah went on to predict the failure of this mission. The outcome would be disastrous, he said. In verse 6, he drove home his point by preaching from the perspective of the animals carrying the diplomats and their plunder through the Negev Desert.

A prophecy concerning the animals of the Negev: Through a land of hardship and distress, of lions and lionesses, of adders and darting snakes, the envoys carry their riches on donkeys' back, their treasures on the humps of camels, to that unprofitable nation, to Egypt, whose help is utterly useless.

He went on in verse 8, telling his listeners to mark his words and record his sermon.

Go now, write it on a tablet for them, inscribe it on a scroll, that for the days to come it may be an everlasting witness. For these are rebellious children, deceitful children, children unwilling to listen to the Lord's instruction.

Not one person, Isaiah complained in verse 10, took seriously his warnings or responded to the sermons of the seers. The word "seer" comes from the term "to see," and it has to do with those who have spiritual insight and foresight. But the people of Jerusalem—from the king down—were in no mood to hear what the prophets had to say.

They say to the seers, "See no more visions!" and to the prophets, "Give us no more visions of what is right!" Tell us pleasant things, prophesy illusions. Leave this way, get off this path, and stop confronting us with the Holy One of Israel."

How relevant to our culture today. This is what our secular society is saying to those of us who are Bible-believing Christians and Bible-preaching ministers: "Stop talking about what is right. If you're going to preach to us, tell us what we want to hear. Stop confronting us with God and with the inspired authority of His Word."

Verse 12 continues—notice Isaiah's vivid language here:

Therefore this is what the Holy One of Israel says: "Because you have rejected this message, relied on oppression, and depended on deceit, this sin will become for you like a high wall, cracked and bulging, that collapses suddenly, in an instant. It will break in pieces like pottery, shattered so mercilessly that among its pieces not a fragment will be found for taking coals from a hearth or scooping water out of a cistern."

In other words, your ungodly lives, strategies, philosophies, and lifestyles will sooner or later collapse like a bulging wall that breaks apart, like a shattering piece of pottery.

And that brings us to our special verse—verse 15—in which hope and compassion return to the prophet's voice, tinged with regret:

> This is what the Sovereign Lord, the Holy One of Israel, says: "In repentance and rest is your salvation, in quietness and trust is your strength, but you would have none of it."

The last phrase of that sentence is stunning—"but you would have none of it." They would have been safe and secure from all alarm had they listened; but they were hell-bent on their own agenda.

This isn't just a message for long-ago Judah. The Lord wants us to see parallels to our own lives. We live in different times from Isaiah, but in many ways not much has changed. We encounter problems every day, and sometimes we feel threatened by circumstances or people who cause us anguish. Sometimes our income isn't sufficient. Sometimes our dreams or schemes don't work. Sometimes our efforts result in apparent failure. Sometimes we battle addictive tendencies. Sometimes we feel exhausted and not in the best spirits. Sometimes we battle depression. Sometimes our health or wealth crumbles. We're prone to seek answers everywhere but from the Lord.

But here in Isaiah 30:15 is a word for times like these. It's a word of timely and quiet strength, and Isaiah spoke this message for you and me just as much as to the inhabitants of ancient Jerusalem. There are four key terms in this verse, all of them related to one another and all of them instructive and wonderful.

REPENTANCE

The first is *repentance*. The verse says, "In repentance and rest is your salvation." In this context, repentance meant recalling the delegation en route to Egypt. For the Judeans and for us, it's turning around in our tracks. Repentance means recognizing we're on the wrong road, wheeling around, and heading in a homeward direction with contrition and humility.

Without repentance there's no rest, quietness, trust, or strength.

In repentance we realize our lives are headed the wrong way. It means we've lost our spiritual calibration but are willing and ready to change. It's as simple as that. When you lose your spiritual calibration, you won't handle the stresses of life well—not until you repent and regain your walk and fellowship with God. That involves stepping away and determining what's wrong. That involves confessing your sin. That means receiving and dedicating or rededicating yourself to the lordship of Christ. We must acknowledge damaging detours, and we must do whatever's necessary to turn our camels around and head toward home, toward God's will for us. You can't tap into the deliverance and strength you need without genuine repentance.

In repentance and rest is your salvation,
in quietness and trust is your strength.

REST

The next word is *rest*. The verse says, "In repentance and rest is your salvation." The word *rest* means that having repented, now you're going to relax and trust God with things. You're going to cast your burdens on the Lord. In biblical usage, the word *rest* doesn't necessarily imply cessation of activity. It simply means you're going to do your best while trusting God with the outcome.

Think of it this way. Your mind is a storeroom filled with boxes, files, containers, and drums. It's cluttered with thousands of assorted thoughts and emotions. These containers are constantly active, always changing. But in the very center of the room is a huge crate. It dominates the room. It fills the middle-most range of the mind. Everything depends on what's in that container. It represents your core thoughts, your center of consciousness, your deepest convictions.

If that box is filled with fear or worry or obsession over problems, you'll suffer debilitation. But if you consciously remove those detrimental things from the box—they may not totally leave your mind; you may box them up and store them on a nearby shelf—but if you take the negative thoughts and emotions out of the central box in the middle of your mind and repack it with the cognizance of the sovereignty of God—then you'll have rest.

Look at this verse again, and notice who is speaking: "This is what the Sovereign Lord, the Holy One of Israel says: 'In repentance and rest is your salvation.'" He is the sovereign Lord. The word *sovereign* is made up of the prefix *sov*, which means all, and *reign*, which means to rule. He rules and reigns over all. The Lord is on His throne. He hasn't abandoned His place in the universe. He knows when a sparrow falls; He numbers the hairs on our heads; He knows the number of our daily footsteps. He rules and reigns, and He is King of kings and Lord of lords.

A friend sent me an email this morning about a pastor who announced he was going to preach a sermon on "God Reigns." But the newspaper misprinted it as "God Resigns." The world acts as if a divine letter of resignation had been posted on heaven's bulletin board. But no; nothing will budge our Lord from His heavenly throne. Nothing can threaten the lordship of Christ. He remains in control of the tides of history and of the ripples that lift us up or cast us down. We can toss our cares on Him. The Bible says, "Cast your cares on the LORD, and he will sustain you" (Ps. 55:22). We have to unpack our anxious cares from that central box and refill it with an awareness of the sovereign power and love and care of Him who died for us, who rose again, and who rules eternally on His throne.

The Bible says, "You will keep him in perfect peace, whose mind is stayed on You, because he trusts in You" (Isa. 26:3 NKJV).

Romans 8:6 says, "The mind governed by the flesh is death, but the mind governed by the Spirit is life and peace."

The Bible says, "If anything is excellent or praiseworthy—think about such things" (Phil. 4:8).

The question isn't, "What's on your mind?" Because we have many things on our minds. The right questions are, "Who is governing your mind? What's at the center of your thoughts? What is at the core of your soul?" When we fill that large core with the sovereignty and holiness of God, well, that's what it means to rest.

The word *rest* is an oft-used biblical term. There's a whole category of "Rest Verses" in the Bible. Let this sampling of them wash through your mind like a refreshing stream.

- *Ask for the ancient paths, ask where the good way is, and walk in it, and you will find **rest** for your souls*—Jeremiah 6:16
- *My Presence will go with you, and I will give you **rest***—Exodus 33:14
- *Truly my soul finds **rest** in God . . . my hope comes from Him*—Psalm 62:1, 5
- *Whoever dwells in the shelter of the Most High will **rest** in the shadow of the Almighty*—Psalm 91:1
- *Come to me, all you who are weary and burdened, and I will give you **rest**. Take my yoke upon you and learn from me, for I am gentle and humble in heart, and you will find **rest** for your souls*—Matthew 11:28–29
- *This is how we know that we belong to the truth and how we set our hearts at **rest** in his presence*—1 John 3:19
- *We who have believed enter that **rest***—Hebrews 4:3
- *In repentance and **rest** is your salvation, in quietness and trust is your strength*—Isaiah 30:15

Anne Cram referred to Isaiah 30:15 in a book of devotions titled *Morning Praise*. Anne grew up in a youth group that memorized Scripture, and now, years later, verses sometimes come to mind unexpectedly. On one occasion she was asked to give a talk at a women's retreat. She tried to gather her thoughts, but, she said, "The butterflies in my stomach started to flap their wings. I prayed for help to calm me down and sort out my thoughts. Immediately came to my mind the words, 'In quietness and in confidence shall be your strength' (Isa. 30:15). Reflecting on this later, I couldn't recall actually learning this verse, and in fact I had to use a concordance to find the reference, but at the time it was just what I needed. Since that day, anytime I have to speak before a crowd of people this verse calms my thoughts and my knocking knees."[3]

QUIETNESS

The third word is *quietness*: "In repentance and rest is your salvation, in quietness and trust is your strength."

Quietness is a condition seldom experienced by modern humanity. It's been that way for awhile now. For example, slow down a moment and read this quotation aloud. See how it strikes you:

> To live a healthy human life in quietness and confidence is not easy in our day. The pace is too rapid; the strain of nerve and muscle is so incessant; the world of thought and opinion has become so large, complex, and baffling; the work of life has become so vast and the day of life so short, that in our struggle to keep the wolf of failure from the door, the demon of worry gets into our heart.[4]

That's an eloquent description of our times; but those words aren't new. They appeared in a publication titled *Good Words for 1888*, and they were penned by a nineteenth-century Edinburgh minister who was expounding on Isaiah 30:15: "In quietness and in confidence shall be your strength."[5]

I'm writing these words on a Saturday night in Sligo, Ireland, where my friend Sam Doherty has just finished speaking at a banquet honoring the work of Child Evangelism Fellowship. Sam, eighty-eight, told us that sixty-five years ago he and his girlfriend were converted to Christ, they were married, and they began the work of CEF in Ireland and became regional directors for all of Europe. Now, sixty-five years later, Sam spoke eloquently of the early days of the work and its incredible growth. When the banquet concluded, I asked him where he got the strength to do all he has done for the last six-and-a-half decades.

"So many times," he said, "I have depended on Isaiah 30:15: 'In quietness and confidence shall be your strength.' I've given that verse to our workers and to others over and over. Quietness is horizontal; it's our attitude toward circumstances and difficulty. Confidence is vertical; it's our trust in God. And when the horizontal and the vertical come together, it becomes inward strength."[6]

Recently I purchased a set of noise-canceling headphones, which are remarkable devices that filter out ambient sounds by creating frequencies that obviate external noises in the ears. It's not simply that the headphones create a soundproof seal. The technology built into them actually reverses or cancels out the sound waves coming at us from all directions, especially noises like conversations, air conditioning, jet engines—things that resemble a constant droning. If we want to listen to music or a lecture, we can turn that on at a lower volume. If we want peace and quiet, we can use the earphones to create a little soundproof zone around us.

But that's just the beginning. There's a company in the UK developing noise-cancelling fences. These aren't just sound-barrier fences like those around a highway or airport; the fencing itself contains technologies that cancel out the noise.[7]

A whole world of technology is opening up in the area of noise-cancellation because too much noise weakens us. It distracts and disturbs us. It drains away our energy, tenses our nerves, and exhausts us.

In the same way, we need noise-cancelling souls. The Bible says God leads us beside still waters (Ps. 23:2). When Jesus said, "Peace, be still" in Mark 4:39, He was speaking to His panicked disciples as much as to the waves and the winds of the storm.

Everyone needs a quiet zone in their lives when they can hear Jesus say, "Peace, be still." It might be a little upstairs desk. Perhaps a rocking chair on the patio or a lawn chair under the weeping willow. Maybe your early morning or late evening times with the Bible at the kitchen table. The secret isn't just cancelling out the ambient sounds; it's listening to the voice of God, which leads to our fourth term: trust.

TRUST

In repentance and rest is your salvation; in
quietness and trust is your strength.

I first learned this verse in the King James Version, and I still like it the best: "In quietness and in confidence shall be your strength."

Confidence is simply a warmer way of expressing the concept of faith. As we repent, rest, find stillness, and exercise confidence, the Lord will strengthen us and show us what to do. Look at Isaiah 30: "Whether you turn to the right or to the left, your ears will hear a voice behind you, saying, 'This is the way; walk in it.'"

The Lord strengthens us with the knowledge of what to do at every point along the way as we trust Him with all our hearts and follow His counsel for our souls. He guides us.

In a letter dated February 13, 1855, the Oxford theologian Bernard Gilpin wrote a friend needing encouragement, and he made a wonderfully simple observation about Isaiah 30:15, which he quoted from the King James Version of the Bible: "'In returning and rest shall ye be saved; in quietness and in confidence shall be your strength;' and it is added, 'ye would not.' You and I know too well what that 'would not' means. Yet I trust there is a spirit given to us which greatly longs after this blessed faith—returning, rest, quietness, confidence. What a progressive sweetness there is in these four words!"[8]

These four words lead to the fifth one, which is the subject of this book: Returning → Rest → Quietness → Confidence → Strength.

Think of the progressive sweetness of those words and mentally circle where you are in the continuum.

Some years ago, I read the biography of a man named W. Eugene Sallee, from Texas, who felt God's calling to missionary service to China. This was in the days when missionaries left home, in all likelihood, never to return. His parents absorbed the news with grace, and they took him to San Francisco where he sailed for Asia aboard the steamship *Coptic*.

Sallee landed in Shanghai, and after some time in orientation, he boarded a river steamer for the interior of that vast, mysterious land. It was unusual, even in those days, for a brand-new missionary to be sent into the interior to begin a new work, but there was something strong and still and confident about Sallee, and he thrived in his work. He was busy from sunup to sundown studying the language, doing evangelistic work, and meeting the needs of those he came to serve. But in the evenings after everyone was quiet, he would retire for personal Bible study. In the spring of 1905, he devoted this time to studying his way through the book of Isaiah, using a handful of cherished commentaries and study aids. On his birthday, he came to Isaiah 30. Here is what he wrote in his diary:

> Amid the shifting scenes of the ancient world, when Assyria and Egypt were struggling for the supremacy of the world, and when all the weaker powers were tempted to ally themselves with either one or the other of these mighty nations, Isaiah came to Judah with this message from the Lord Jehovah, the Holy One of Israel, "In returning and rest shall ye be

saved; in quietness and in confidence shall be your strength." This is my birthday. I am twenty-seven years old today. Let this be my birthday text. O my soul. Thou desirest strength. Seek it not from the Egyptians, nor from the Assyrians, nor from any of the world powers, but return thou to the Holy One of Israel, rest in Him, for in quietness and confidence shall be thy strength.[9]

That birthday verse became a beloved text in his heart and served as a motto for his lifetime of purpose and productivity. It can be our text too. When we look to the Lord in repentance and rest and quietness and confidence, He imparts a strength from beyond ourselves, from beyond the stars, from the very throne of God.

Your strength will equal your days, for the eyes of the Lord range around the world to strengthen those whose hearts are fully committed to Him. He is our refuge and strength, and His joy is the strength of our lives. In returning and rest we will be saved; and in quietness and confidence is your strength. We can stand like a giant sequoia above the commotion of the wildwoods.

A WORD FROM KATRINA

In quietness and trust is your strength—Isaiah 30:15.

This is difficult for me because I verbalize my frustrations. I'm not quiet; in fact, I can grumble, shout, holler, yell, complain, and scream with the rest of them. My disability creates a lot of unexpected trials during the course of every day; they catch me unawares all the time. And it's easy to become upset. I think everyone is prone to be upset nowadays. We live in a world of pressure, whatever our situation.

It helps me settle down and regain composure, however, whenever I think of Jesus as a Lamb. That's a very poignant picture in my mind. There are a lot of Bible verses about quietness, calmness, and stillness; and I love them all. But somehow it's my mental images of the serenity of Jesus that help me most. His words were never out of control, and my motivation is to be like Him.

SIX

Catch Updrafts Like an Eagle

Those who hope in the Lord will renew their strength.

ISAIAH 40:31

In today's world, renewable energy is the fuel of tomorrow's economy. When we pump a barrel of oil or dig a ton of coal out of the ground, it comes from a finite supply. The world's underground deposits—though vast—are reduced by that barrel or ton. But when we capture the same amount of energy by a solar panel, a wind turbine, or a waterfall, it doesn't reduce the sun or the wind or the river one bit.

Hence, it's renewable.

Just think of the wonders of solar power, for instance. High above our heads is a massive star, the sun, a gigantic atomic reactor providing enough power in one minute to supply all the world's energy needs for an entire year.[1] It sounds simple. But flip-flopping the world's energy sources is, well, a hot topic. It's not easy to convert an entire planet from carbon fuels to sustainable power in a short period of time. Wars are fought over these issues, economies can be wrecked, and political campaigns won or lost.

Before you think renewable energy is a new discovery, let me tell you about my grandfather, Rev. W. L. Morgan. He knew about renewable energy a hundred years ago. There's a spot on our family property in Tennessee called the Old Mill Place. That's where my granddad had a waterwheel to grind the neighbors' corn. He harnessed the energy of the rushing creek as effectively as modern engineers switch on hydroelectric dams, resulting in the sweet smell of cornbread wafting up and down the hollows.

My grandfather, who was a mountain evangelist, knew something else too. He understood the spiritual side of renewable energy, which is as old as the Bible and as ancient as the human soul. God, as it were, created waterwheels in our hearts and windmills in our minds to catch the living waters and the fresh winds of the Spirit. He put solar reactors within us, aimed at the Son of God.

Jesus called Himself the Light of the World (John 8:12). Ephesians 5:14 says He shines on us. The prophet Malachi said, "For you who revere my name, the sun of righteousness will rise with healing in its rays" (Mal. 4:2). When the apostle John saw the glorified Christ in Revelation 1:16, he said, "His face was like the sun shining in all its brilliance." And the psalmist said, "The LORD God is a sun and shield; the LORD bestows favor and honor; no good thing does he withhold from those whose walk is blameless" (Ps. 84:11).

That includes renewable strength for each day's needs. To stay energized in life, we need to soak up the heavenly sunlight and harness the fresh wind and quickening currents of the Spirit. We can draw perpetual strength from Him without ever diminishing or lessening His omnipotence by a single kilowatt.

That brings us to our next power line in the Bible, the hallowed promise at the end of Isaiah 40: "Those who hope in the LORD will renew their strength. They will soar on wings like eagles; They will run and not grow weary, they will walk and not be faint" (v. 31).

HERE IS YOUR GOD

This is Hebrew poetry at its finest, but the phrases aren't just floating in thin air like cirrus clouds. They're as real as a refugee crisis.

Here's the background. The last section of Isaiah, chapters 40–66, was initially written to comfort Jewish refugees in Babylon who had been dislocated five hundred miles from Jerusalem. As I write this, the newspapers are full of heart-wrenching stories of the waves of refugees from the Middle East flooding into Europe, drowning in the Mediterranean, and being turned back at the Hungarian border.

In Old Testament days, the nation of Judah faced a refugee crisis of another sort and just as traumatic. Having survived the Assyrian invasion of the early 700s BC (as we saw in the last two chapters), the Israeli nation finally fell to the Babylonian empire in 587 BC. The city of Jerusalem went up in flames and the Jewish temple collapsed in rubble. Many people were killed, and most of the grieving survivors were force-marched more than five hundred miles to refugee settlements in Babylon, in modern-day Iraq. These camps became semi-permanent as the decades passed, and tents gave way to buildings. The Hebrews forgot their hymns, hung their harps on the willow trees, and mourned the loss of their temple, sacrifices, and homeland. But they never lost hope, for the prophet Jeremiah had predicted a return within seventy years.

Sure enough, seventy years after the initial wave of Babylonian incursions, King Cyrus of Persia, the new kid on the block, issued a decree allowing some of the Jews to return to their homeland. The story of the returnees is told in the books of Ezra and Nehemiah. It was a rigorous, thankless trip, for they had to try to reclaim territory now held by their enemies and rebuild a city destroyed by their foes. They needed the strongest encouragement possible. They needed strength to keep them running without weariness and walking without fainting. They needed unlimited supplies of renewable energy.

Isaiah 40–66 was addressed to these returnees and for those who, unable to return themselves, were sending them.

I believe Isaiah, who lived in the earlier days of the Assyrian crisis, was enabled by the Holy Spirit to address these chapters to a generation living after him. He spoke to them as though he were among them, as though he were their contemporary. The last twenty-seven chapters of his book are, in essence, a miracle of inspiration. Isaiah was empowered to write to the returning Jewish exiles as though he actually lived among them, even though his lifespan occurred more than a century earlier.

These chapters are full of tenderness, reassurance, comfort, messianic hope, and unquenchable optimism, and that's why we love them so much today. If you're in a prolonged slump, study these chapters. One chapter a day will take you through the entire twenty-seven chapters in a month, with a few extra days for review.

The opening chapter in this section, Isaiah 40, is arguably the richest passage of Scripture for helping us visualize the majesty of God. It begins with "comfort" and ends on "wings like eagles." In between is a description of God unequalled in Scripture.

Notice how the chapter begins with its double use of the word *comfort* and the adjectives *my* and *your*, and with an emphasis on tenderness:

> Comfort, comfort my people, says your God. Speak tenderly to Jerusalem, and proclaim to her that her hard service has been completed. . . . A voice of one calling: "In the wilderness prepare the way for the Lord; make straight in the desert a highway for our God. Every valley shall be raised up, every mountain and hill made low; the rough ground shall become level, the rugged places a plain. And the glory of the Lord will be revealed, and all people will see it together. For the mouth of the Lord has spoken." (vv. 1–5)

Isaiah proceeded to remind his readers of the unbreakable nature of Scripture.

The grass withers and the flowers fall, but the word of our God endures forever. (v. 8)

Then in verse 9, he came to his thesis, his great encouragement:

You who bring good news to Zion, go up on a high mountain. You who bring good news to Jerusalem, lift up your voice with a shout, lift it up, do not be afraid; say to the towns of Judah, "Here is your God!"

Here is your God! For seventy years, the Jewish people felt they had abandoned God—or had been abandoned by Him. Now Isaiah was shouting from the mountaintops: Here is your God! Rediscover Him! Recover your vision of Him! Look at Him! Study Him! Ponder Him! Think of His greatness! Find comfort in His presence!

Isaiah was describing something just as available to you and me as to the Jewish refugees: "I have a message of comfort to those who have been distressed, displaced, and discouraged in life. God has forgiven everything in the past, and He's putting you on a pathway of straight roads and level highways, revealing His glory and keeping His eternal promises. It's time to climb to the summit and shout good news to the world. It's time to cast away your fear. It's time to realize: here is your God!"

This is biblical comfort. If you feel displaced or discouraged, here is your God. If you've been lonely, far removed from love and laughter, here is your God. If you're heartbroken or downcast, here is your God.

With that we forge into the rest of chapter 40, which offers a descriptive series of images portraying the God who comes to our aid. The last half of Isaiah 40 is arguably the Bible's most majestic series of pictures depicting the practical power of our sovereign Lord. These are words to read, to revisit often, to convert to praise and prayer, to visualize, and to memorize.[2]

Isaiah presented these pictures through a set of rhetorical questions, beginning with the first phrase of verse 12: "Who has measured the waters in the hollow of his hand . . . ?"

The hollow of one's hand is the little bowl formed by cupping the palm. How much water can it hold? I performed a little experiment to see how many tablespoons of water I could hold in the hollow of my hand. I thought maybe two or three; but when I poured in just one tablespoon some of the liquid overflowed and fell into the sink. Our hands are very small. Our capacity is limited. But the Bible says God can, as it were, hold all the waters of all the oceans in the hollow of His hand.

Look at His outstretched hand, marked with a nail print, reaching out and forming a cup. Take the Pacific and pour it into the hollow of His hand. That's the largest ocean by far, covering over one-fourth of the entire planet and equal in size to nearly all the land area on earth. At its deepest point, it descends to more than 35,000 feet. Then pour in the Atlantic, which ties together Africa, Europe, the Americas and the Caribbean, the Mediterranean, and the Black Sea. Add the Indian Ocean, the Southern Ocean, and the Arctic Ocean. Drain all of the oceans of the earth into the hollow of His hand and not a drop will overflow. That's the size of the hand holding and helping us. He measures the waters in the hollow of His hand, and a chapter later we read: "I will uphold you with my righteous right hand . . . For I am the LORD your God who takes hold of your right hand and says to you, Do not fear; I will help you" (Isa. 41:10, 13).

Verse 12 goes on to tell us what God does with His other hand: "Who has measured the waters in the hollow of his hand, or with the breadth of his hand marked off the heavens?"

The breadth of your hand is the space between the end of your thumb and the end of your smallest finger. I measured mine. It's about eight inches and I can't even get it around a cola can. According to this verse, the Lord can reach out and cover the entire universe with the span of His hand. For thousands of years, people have looked into the night sky and wondered about the size of the universe. The early astronomers discovered we were just looking at a tiny portion of one corner of the universe, which came to be called the Milky Way. In 1924, Edwin Hubble suggested there could be many other galaxies beyond the Milky Way, and now we know there are billions of galaxies. Scientists are currently speculating on whether ours is the only universe or if there could be other universes beyond our own. The size of the cosmos boggles our minds; and yet to the Lord it represents nothing more than the span of His hand.

But verse 12 isn't finished. There's another question: "Who has held the dust of the earth in a basket . . . ?"

How much dirt can you carry in a pail? Take a five-gallon bucket and fill it with dirt. Can you carry it? What about one in each hand? How far could you haul those buckets? Fly down the Atlantic seaboard from Myrtle Beach to Miami. Look at all the sand and imagine how many grains there are. Drive through the Mojave Desert from Las Vegas to Los Angeles and try to count the dunes. The Lord can carry all the sand and dust and dirt on earth like a child carrying a sand bucket at the beach.

Verse 12 poses another question: "Who has . . . weighed the mountains on the scales and the hills in a balance?"

I have a pair of bathroom scales, which go up to 300 or 350 pounds; I'm about 170, so I'm not sure its maximum capacity. But imagine dropping Mount Everest onto those scales. Scientists would love to know its weight because we don't know if it's hollow in the middle, being volcanic. But don't stop with Everest. Let's pile on all the Himalayas, the greatest mountain chain on earth. It stretches across South Asia and includes more than one hundred mountains close to the size of Mount Everest. Stack the Andes on top and throw in the Alps, the Rocky Mountains, and the Sierra Madres. For good measure, top it all off with my native Appalachians. All the mountain ranges in the world added together don't register more than an ounce or so on the scales of God.

Verses 13 and 14 go on to ask: "Who can fathom the Spirit of the Lord, or instruct the Lord as his counselor? Whom did the Lord consult to enlighten him, and who taught him the right way? Who was it that taught him knowledge, or showed him the path of understanding?"

What university did God attend? Where did He get His education? Who mentored Him? The answer: no one. God is the source and center of all knowledge and wisdom. He can teach but He cannot learn, for He instantly and instinctively knows every detail of reality, everywhere and at every time.

Verse 15 adds another incredible depiction: "Surely the nations are like a drop in the bucket . . ."

There are more than two hundred nations in the world right now (depending on who's counting), and some are causing a lot of trouble, waging wars, oppressing peoples, and threatening civilizations. Jesus predicted the last days would be characterized by wars and rumors of war. We're gripped by earth's geopolitics, and our technology allows us instant updates from every corner of the globe. But in God's sight, the entire lot of nations is like a drop in the bucket.

After watering your potted plants, turn the watering can over and notice the few drops that fall out. That's what the nations of the world are like compared to the sovereign reign of almighty God. From His unchanging throne, He's seen empires and emperors come and go, rulers live and die, nations rise and fall—one after another. His kingdom is an everlasting kingdom, and the nations are like spare drops from an upended bucket.

Verses 21–22 are some of the most beautiful words in the Bible: "Do you not know? Have you not heard? Has it not been told you from the beginning? Have you not understood since the earth was founded? He sits enthroned above the circle of the earth, and its people are like grasshoppers. He stretches out the heavens like a canopy, and spreads them out like a tent to live in."

Notice that phrase: "the circle of the earth." In medieval days, people claimed the world was flat. But the Bible told us in the days of Isaiah it was a great circle, a great sphere. And the heavens are stretched around it like a canopy or tent, providing a beautiful environment in which we can live.

Years ago, our family used to go camping, and we named our tent BLT—the Brave Little Tent—because of all the rainstorms it endured. But the Bible says the entire universe is like a tent God pitched around the sphere of our planet in order to show us His glory.

Isaiah compared human beings to grasshoppers. Think of the men and women now occupying the leadership of the nations of the world. You see their faces every day, hear their boasts, watch them struggle for power, see the ruin of their mistakes. They live in palaces, fly in helicopters, drive in motorcades, live like kings, and make decisions like playing chess. But in God's sight they're like a bunch of grasshoppers, jumping around with antennae out, eyes wide, legs tucked in, leaping in alarm when the grass trembles.

Verses 23–24 say: "He brings princes to naught and reduces the rulers of this world to nothing. No sooner are they planted, no sooner are they sown, no sooner do they take root in the ground, than he blows on them and they wither, and a whirlwind sweeps them away like chaff."

Beginning in Isaiah 40:25 we come to another set of rhetorical questions so eloquent in their wording we should read them aloud: "'To whom will you compare me? Or who is my equal?' says the Holy One. Lift up your eyes and look to the heavens: Who created all these? He who brings out the starry host one by one and calls forth each of them by name. Because of his great power and mighty strength, not one of them is missing (vv. 25–26)."

God, wanting to astonish and thrill us, created too many stars in the sky to count. The aforementioned Milky Way is home to about 300 billion stars, and astronomers estimate there are another 100 billion galaxies. The known cosmos seems endless and we don't know its parameters or dimensions. But just imagine: 100 billion galaxies, each with 300 billion stars—and that's a conservative count: 3,000,000,000,000,000,000,000.

Yet God knows every solitary star, and each has a name on His stellar map. He enjoys them one by one and calls them each by name. Furthermore, He knows every statistic about every star, sun, moon, planet, asteroid, comet, supernova, pulsar, nebula, and meteor. He knows the facts intimately.

If that is true, why should we fear He can't keep up with us? Verse 27 asks: "Why do you complain, Jacob? Why do you say, Israel, 'My way is hidden from the Lord; my cause is disregarded by my God'?"

If our God is able to keep track of a billion galaxies, each containing billions of stars, don't you think He can keep up with you and your handful of concerns? If He knows the flight plan of every sparrow, don't you think He knows your circumstances? If He instantly comprehends every need in every corner of His vast cosmos, how can you worry He's forgotten about you and your need for strength today?

> Do you not know? Have you not heard? The LORD is the everlasting God, the Creator of the ends of the earth. He will not grow tired or weary, and his understanding no one can fathom. He gives strength to the weary and increases the power of the weak. Even youths grow tired and weary, and young men stumble and fall; but those who hope in the LORD will renew their strength. They will soar on wings like eagles. (Isa. 40: 28–31)

As if we've not had enough imagery in this chapter, here Isaiah added another visualization—eagles. Eagles are majestic birds with remarkable vision. Their eyes are larger than human eyes, and scientists believe their eyesight may be eight times sharper than ours. They have the kind of telescopic vision we attribute to superheroes. Eagles also have powerful feet with talons that can grip like a vice. Their beaks are as sharp as a butcher knife, designed to cut and crush and tear their food.

But most of all, an eagle is built for flying. They soar at incredible speeds, flying at sixty and eighty and one hundred miles an hour. Like a stunt plane, they can do rolls and loops and dives and flips. Their wingspan extends nearly eight feet, but they don't fly like a sparrow or robin or hummingbird. They seldom flap their wings. Eagles are built for soaring, which allows them to travel vast distances on very little energy.

God created our planet with invisible columns of hot air called thermals rising up here and there from the ground. Eagles know how to find these thermals, fly into their invisible currents, stretch out their wings, and catch the updraft. They're lifted higher and higher into the sky as though ascending on an elevator. They may rise as high as fifteen thousand feet—so high in the heavens they cannot be seen with the naked eye from earth.

When they reach those heights, they emerge from the thermal column, their wings still spread, and soar this way and that way, downward and sideward and upward, traveling for miles with very little exertion of strength. They don't frantically flap their wings; they simply stretch them out and catch the updrafts of God's thermals.

This is Isaiah's picture of faith. If you need strength for your journey, you have to stretch out the wings of faith and catch the updrafts of the promises of God. You don't have to flutter and flap around. You can rest on the uplifting promises of God. You can find your strength in Him, and it's exhilarating.

I've done this many times. When I find my stomach getting knotted over some problem, I sneak away, open my Bible, and search until I find the needed promise, which arises from the page like a thermal column. Then I spread out my wings and catch the updraft. I can show you countless verses and passages I've highlighted, underlined, circled, copied into my journal, and inscribed on my mind. Sometimes I have to force my mind to move from the problem to the promise, but whenever I do I'm able to catch the updraft of God's grace.

While proofing this chapter, I thumbed through some old journals stored atop my bookshelf. I came across an entry for October 15, 1981:

Nashville—I've been in a bleak mood tonight but have been reading a chapter in a book by evangelist John R. Rice in which he wrote about Isaiah 40, that those who wait upon the Lord shall renew their strength. Rice said, "God is never discouraged . . . God is never tired . . . God is never at His wits end . . . God is never at the end of His understanding, never at the limit of His wisdom. . . . They that wait upon the Lord shall renew their strength." Dear Lord, at the close of this day with its pressures and disappointments I recall Your words and wish to have the attitude of waiting upon You. Thank You for never getting discouraged, not even with me.[3]

I can't recall what was troubling me that evening so long ago, but I found an updraft that lifted my spirits and relaxed my mind so I could sleep.

As he pressed toward the end of chapter 40, Isaiah expanded the lesson beyond soaring. People who learn this practice, he said, gain so much strength they "will run and not grow weary, they will walk and not be faint" (v. 31).

Once in a private conversation, Ruth Bell Graham compared Psalm 55:6 ("Oh, that I had the wings of a dove! I would fly away and be at rest") with Isaiah 40:31 ("Those who hope in the LORD will renew their strength. They will soar on wings like eagles"). She gave me her philosophy of vacations. Some people, she said, race off to escape the pressure and usually fly back exhausted. But when we learn to take a spiritual break by resting and waiting on the Lord, we'll mount up with wings like eagles. She said she tried to design vacations for her and her husband that resulted in their returning spiritually and physically refreshed, ready for the next assignment.[4]

One day I spoke on Isaiah 40 to a group in Texas. Afterward my friend, Shirley Horn, approached me. "That's my verse," she said.

Many years before, when she was young and just starting out in adult life, she overextended herself and came to a point of exhausted depression. Her spirits were about to cave in like a mineshaft riddled with rotten timber. She walked out of her house in Coronado Village, ambled absently down the street, and turned at the intersection. She wanted to give up.

As she rounded the corner, she looked up. There—high in the sky, soaring over the edge of town—was an enormous bird with a broad wingspan. Shirley didn't know what kind of bird—an eagle? A hawk? It glided with carefree abandon.

Suddenly a phrase came into Shirley's mind—Isaiah 40:31: "Those who wait upon the Lord will renew their strength. They will mount up with wings like eagles." Shirley told me the rush of those words was like an uplifting wind that instantly renewed her strength. The funny thing was she wasn't aware of having ever before seen that verse. Perhaps on some earlier occasion she'd heard it quoted and it landed in her subconscious mind.

At any rate, on this occasion it came to her word-perfect and the effect was immediate. "From that day," she told me, "that has been my verse for life. I can still see myself walking and looking into the sky that day; it's so vivid in my memory. I just knew God brought that scripture to my mind the instant I saw that bird soaring on the currents so high up. I immediately began to thank Him over and over, and I had an awesome sense of peace from that moment. What a blessing!"[5]

It's all summed up in one verse in the next chapter—Isaiah 41:10, which is a strength verse I memorized in childhood: "Do not fear, for I am with you; do not be dismayed, for I am your God. I will strengthen you and help you. I will uphold you with my righteous right hand."

If you're a little bewildered by your load today, remember the words of Isaiah—*Here is your God!*—and tap into His renewable energy. Contemplate Him and the specific promises He gives in times of need. Catch the updrafts of His grace on the wings of faith.

Why do you complain, Jacob? Why do you say, Israel, "My way is hidden from the Lord; my cause is disregarded by my God"? Do you not know? Have you not heard? The Lord is the everlasting God, the Creator of the ends of the earth. He will not grow tried or weary, and his understanding no one can fathom. He gives strength to the weary and increases the power of the weak. Even youths grow tired and weary, and young men stumble and fall; but those who hope in the Lord will renew their strength. They will soar on wings like eagles; they will run and not grow weary, they will walk and not be faint. (Isa. 40:27–31)

A WORD FROM KATRINA

This has been one of my favorite verses for a long time. I created a little song so I wouldn't forget it, using my own made-up melody. My version of the Bible uses the "wait" on the Lord, so I use that word. Here's the way I sing it:

> *They that wait upon the Lord shall renew their strength (repeat).*
> *They shall mount up with wings as eagles;*
> *They shall run and not be weary.*
> *They shall mount up with wings as eagles;*
> *They shall walk and not faint.*
> *They that wait upon the Lord shall renew their strength (repeat).*

There are few days when I don't sing this song to my heart. When I wait on the Lord, my mind centers on Him, not on my weakness. God is waiting on my waiting; He has not given me a spirit of fear, dread, discouragement, or failure, but of power and love and of a sound mind (2 Tim. 1:7).

Hope lifts; it smashes discouragement, it stimulates faith, and it puts me on the right track. Try turning this verse into a song for yourself. It'll be like wind beneath your wings.

SEVEN

Strengthen Someone Else

The Lord will . . . satisfy your needs in a
sun-scorched land and will strengthen your frame.

ISAIAH 58:11

Afellow once went up to my friend Alan Graham of Northern Ireland and asked him what he was doing with his life. "I'm building a business," replied Alan, "and raising a family, making a living, and building a home."

The man said, "Why don't you give it all up and come to County Donegal in the northwest of Ireland and tell boys and girls about Jesus Christ, because no one is telling them?"

Those words struck Alan like stones from a slingshot. After considerable thought and prayer, Alan and his wife, Dorothy, left their comfortable life in Belfast and joined the ranks of a wonderful organization called Child Evangelism Fellowship. They began spreading the gospel among schoolchildren in Ireland. Some years later, Alan traveled to Romania for CEF, and for the first time he came face to face with extreme poverty. This was shortly before the fall of Communism, and shortages were rampant. Alan saw naked children living in open wagons with snow falling on them. He saw families without food and shelter. Deeply distressed, he began researching what the Bible taught about feeding the poor, clothing the naked, and caring for the needy.

Alan was particularly drawn to Isaiah 58, one of the Bible's great humanitarian chapters. The truths expressed in this and other biblical passages changed his life. As a result, Alan and Dorothy ended up in Zimbabwe, where, one frightening day as they returned from teaching school in an impoverished area, a hostile mob of 120 angry soldiers swarmed their truck and began rocking it from side to side, chanting and shouting political slogans and terrible threats.

"We're going to die!" screamed Dorothy.

Alan got out of the truck and felt the barrel of a gun pressed into his neck.

I'll finish the story later, but suffice to say, Isaiah 58 isn't for the faint of heart. It can take you into war zones, boondocks, and soup kitchens. It can push you out the door with a basket of groceries for strangers across town. It can introduce you to orphans and underprivileged children. It's an eloquent set of pleas and promises proffered by God to His people about penetrating the impoverished corners and corridors of society.

Though I've studied the Bible for decades, I had never lingered in this chapter until studying the strength passages of the Bible. I don't actually remember having ever read Isaiah 58, though I've read through the Bible on several occasions. Now, having drilled into this chapter, I can understand its effect on people like Alan Graham. It should be required reading for every one of us, for its message is as relevant now as when it was first written.

The subject of Isaiah 58 is fasting, which, to us, means abstaining from food for a period of time mainly for purposes of prayer and spiritual discipline. It's not the most popular topic in Scripture, but Isaiah took a singular approach to the subject.

THE WRONG KIND OF FAST (VERSES 1–5)

He began the chapter by accusing the people of his day of practicing the wrong kind of fast. It's true they were fasting. They were doing so more diligently than most of us. The people of Judah had developed routines to their religion. They had implemented pious habits into their schedule. As you know, it's not easy to alter our schedules. Try rearranging your calendar to include time for exercise or some other new habit. It's challenging to revise well-trodden routines, but Judeans had done it. They had set aside time for fasting. They had mastered their appetites and designated certain periods for self-denial and hunger pangs. Not many of us have successfully implemented a system of fasting in our lives. I confess I haven't. The people of Judah did that, but there was a problem. Their routines were mere rituals. Nothing more.

This is the dangerous thing about Judaism and Christianity. By its very nature, Christianity depends on a series of holy habits. The Bible describes the Christian life as a "walk," and that implies habitual behaviors. We read our Bibles, pray, and perhaps memorize Scripture. We go to church on Sundays. We give our tithes. We pray before meals. We have our daily devotions. Perhaps we even periodically fast.

These routines serve as the tracks or the grooves for our relationship with the Lord. I cherish the spiritual disciplines that give structure to my faith. Routines and habits help internalize our beliefs and behavior. But it's easy for the real meaning of our habits to fade away until they become facades, nothing more than scaffolding around fake walls like a movie set. Even though I'm a pastor, I have to make sure I'm not just going through the motions. On Sundays during our worship services, for example, I often look up at the ceiling and imagine we have a cutaway roof that opens up to heaven itself and we are worshipping around the very throne of God. I want to stay tuned into reality as I worship. Yet it's easy to sing a hymn or praise song while my mind is thinking of something else.

This is the deadening danger Isaiah wanted to confront, and he used the example of fasting. Notice how the Lord directed him to begin his sermon in chapter 58:

> Shout it aloud, do not hold back. Raise your voice like a trumpet. Declare to my people their rebellion and to the descendants of Jacob their sins. For day after day they seek me out; they seem eager to know my ways, as if they were a nation that does what is right and has not forsaken the commands of its God. They ask me for just decisions and seem eager for God to come near them. (vv. 1–2)

On the surface, the Israelites seemed like a spiritual people. Judah appeared as a religious nation, eager to know God's ways and acting as if it wanted to do what was right. But there was little reality to their devotion. According to Isaiah, the people themselves knew something was missing. Their routines yielded sparse satisfaction and few answered prayers. They asked in verse 3:

> Why have we fasted . . . and you have not seen it? Why have we humbled ourselves, and you have not noticed?

In the same verse, the Lord answered their question, explaining:

> On the day of your fasting, you do as you please and exploit all your workers. Your fasting ends in quarreling and strife, and in striking each other with wicked fists. (vv. 3–4)

Even while they were fasting, they were taking advantage of those beneath them. They were abusive. They were exploitative. They underpaid their employees. And they were in a bad mood; they went from fasting to fisticuffs. Their spiritual rituals didn't make them any easier to live with. Isaiah continued in verses 4–5:

You cannot fast as you do today and expect your voice to be heard on high. Is this the kind of fast I have chosen, only a day for people to humble themselves? Is it only for bowing one's head like a reed and for lying in sackcloth and ashes? Is that what you call a fast, a day acceptable to the LORD?

During fast days, the Judeans appeared to humble themselves. They bowed their heads like reeds in the breeze. They put on sackcloth and ashes. Yet even during their fasting, they took advantage of their workers. They didn't pay adequate wages. They misused the poor. They lacked the compassionate spirit of Yahweh. They got into quarrels. "That's the wrong way to fast," warned Isaiah. It reminds me of something I once heard: when we become Christians, our husbands, wives, children, coworkers, and even our dog or cat should be able to tell the difference.

THE RIGHT KIND OF FAITH (VERSES 6–7)

Beginning in verse 6, Isaiah turned the tables and described the kind of fast the Lord truly desires and the right kind of faith. This is the kind of religion we should practice to truly please God.

Is not this the kind of fasting I have chosen: to loose the chains of injustice . . . to set the oppressed free and break every yoke?

Isaiah proceeded to preach a wonderful sermon here about benevolence and humanitarianism. As I studied it, it reminded me of what the epistle of James says about how true religion cares for the orphans and widows (James 1:27). Correcting oppression and injustice—that's the kind of fast and the kind of faith God desires. We're to abstain from selfishness, greed, harshness, and hard-heartedness.

True religion has always carried the poor on its back. As I indicated in an earlier chapter, this is what Christianity has done for two thousand years. We care for people. We care about racial justice. We care about adequate wages. We care about malnutrition. We care about disease. We care for those in prison. We care for the illiterate. We care about clean water, unborn children, and empty stomachs. We give our money to help them. We share our time and energy to minister to them in ways that meet tangible needs. This is what we do—the Bible calls it "good works"—and this is what the world notices.

Dr. Paul Maier of Western Michigan University put it eloquently in the foreword of Alvin J. Schmidt's book *How Christianity Changed the World:*

> Even knowledgeable believers will be amazed at how many of our pres-ent institutions and values reflect a Christian origin. Not only countless individual lives but civilization itself was transformed by Jesus Christ. In the ancient world, His teachings elevated brutish standards of morality, halted infanticide, enhanced human life, emancipated women, abolished slavery, inspired charities and relief organizations, created hospitals, established orphanages, and founded schools.
>
> In medieval times, Christianity almost single-handedly kept classical culture alive through recopying manuscripts, building libraries, moder-ating warfare through truce days, and providing dispute arbitrations.
>
> It was Christians who invented colleges and universities, dignified labor as a divine vocation, and extended the light of civilization to bar-barians on the frontiers . . .
>
> The faith can be splendidly defended on . . . its record of being *the* most powerful agent in transforming society for the better across two thousand years since Jesus lived on the earth . . . No other religion, philosophy, teaching, nation, movement—whatever—has so changed the world for the better as Christianity has done.[1]

Who have been at the forefront of orphan care? Reforming child labor laws? Abolishing slavery? Fighting sex trafficking? Defending pre-born children? Developing schools and hospitals? Providing shelters for the homeless? Mobilizing relief during natural disasters? Drilling for water? Caring for refugees? Risking their lives to fight disease?

The whole world followed the story of the brave band of medical workers who confronted the Ebola virus in West Africa. Dr. Kent Brantly, for example, was on duty there when the virus spun out of control. He sent his family out of the area, but he continued treating the sick at his station. In the process, he contracted the very disease he was trying to fight. He was flown to America aboard a special quarantine medical aircraft and treated at Emory University, where, thankfully, he recovered. Upon his release he spoke at a news conference, saying, "As a medical missionary, I never imagined myself in this position. When my family and I moved to Liberia last October to begin a two-year term working with Samaritan's Purse, Ebola was not on the radar. We moved to Liberia because God called us to serve the people of Liberia."

He explained how the crisis began and the wrenching decision to send his family out of the country while he remained.

"After taking Amber and our children to the airport to return to the States on Sunday morning, July 20, I poured myself into my work even more than before—transferring patients to our new, bigger isolation unit; training and orienting new staff; and working with our Human Resources officer to fill our staffing needs. Three days later, on Wednesday, July 23, I woke up feeling under the weather, and then my life took an unexpected turn as I was diagnosed with Ebola Virus Disease. As I lay in my bed in Liberia for the following nine days, getting sicker and weaker each day, I prayed that God would help me to be faithful even in my illness, and I prayed that in my life or in my death, He would be glorified."

Brantly continued, "I have learned since that there were thousands, maybe even millions of people around the world praying for me throughout that week, and even still today. And I have heard story after story of how this situation has impacted the lives of individuals around the globe—both among my friends and family, and also among complete strangers. I cannot thank you enough for your prayers and your support. But what I can tell you is that I serve a faithful God who answers prayers."[2]

This is what Isaiah was preaching about. One of the reasons I'm thankful to be a Christ follower is because no other group on earth has ever changed the world for good like those committed to the gospel. Jesus cared for the sick, touched the dead, healed the lepers, forgave the sinners, rebuked the greedy, and did so without neglecting the eternal dimensions of His mission. He was a walking, living embodiment of Isaiah 58. His followers are—or should be—the same.

Verses 6 and 7 continue Isaiah's theme:

Is not this the kind of fasting I have chosen . . . ? Is it not to share your food with the hungry and to provide the poor wanderer with shelter—when you see the naked, to clothe them, and not to turn away from your own flesh and blood?

I believe Christians are the world's truest humanitarians. Recently I spoke to a group connected with the Texas Baptist Men, an organization that mobilizes during natural emergencies to bring help and hope to the suffering. One of their ministries is providing clean water in needy areas. Much of the disease in the developing world is the result of impure water, which causes the deaths of approximately eighteen hundred children every day. According to UNICEF, if ninety school buses filled with preschoolers crashed every day with no survivors, the world would notice. Yet that's how many young children perish daily from impure water and inadequate sanitation.[3]

One of the Texas men, Harold Patterson, is a mechanic with a tremendous burden for providing clean water in needy areas. Early in his career,

Patterson had worked on an oil well-drilling rig, and the experience led him to design a simple, low-cost, automated water-drilling rig that can be disassembled in four pieces, packed in boxes, and loaded onto an airplane anywhere in the world. Once in country, it's reassembled. It can drill a hundred feet and tap into a safe water supply. It takes two people to deliver the equipment, set it up, dig the well, and train local people how to use it. The Texas Baptist Men sends out teams with these contraptions, and they dig the wells, train local Christians, and then leave the drilling units behind so wells can be dug in other places.

This is what Christians do. This is the right kind of fast and the right kind of faith. It reaches out to the needs of a hurting world.

THE BEST KIND OF BLESSINGS (VERSES 8–11)

The most beautiful section of the chapter is still to come. Having talked about the wrong kind of fast and the right kind of faith, Isaiah ended his message by describing the best kind of blessings—what God will do in the lives of those who reflect His mercy.

Then your light will break forth like the dawn, and your healing will quickly appear; then your righteousness will go before you, and the glory of the Lord will be your rear guard. Then you will call, and the Lord will answer; you will cry for help, and he will say: Here am I.

If you do away with the yoke of oppression, with the pointing finger and malicious talk, and if you spend yourselves in behalf of the hungry and satisfy the needs of the oppressed, then your light will rise in the darkness, and your night will become like the noonday.

The Lord will guide you always; he will satisfy your needs in a sun-scorched land and will strengthen your frame. You will be like a well-watered garden, like a spring whose waters never fail.

As I analyzed this passage, I numbered ten different benefits that flood into the lives of those who exercise the right kind of compassionate faith.

First, your light will break forth like the dawn (v. 8). You'll be a bright and luminescent person, and the sunlight of the gospel will glow from your life.

Second, your healing will quickly appear (v. 8). You'll be able to stay emotionally healthy and look forward to eternal health and strength.

Third, the Lord will go before you and behind you (v. 8). He will mop up all the problems of your yesterdays and precede into all the potential of your tomorrows. This reminds me of Psalm 139:5, which says, "You both precede and follow me and place your hand of blessing on my head" (TLB).

Fourth, the Lord will answer your prayers (v. 9). When you call, He will say, "Here I am!"

Fifth, your light will rise in the darkness and your night will become like the noonday (v. 10). You'll be noticed; you'll have influence; in the darkness of this world, you'll make a difference. The world will see your good deeds and glorify your Father in heaven.

Sixth, the Lord will guide you always (v. 11). He will show you what to do and help you with your decisions. I once listened to a young lady—a teenager—who had been rescued from certain death as an infant in the Ukraine and adopted and raised by a missionary family. During her testimony she made a statement so compelling I pulled out my pen and paper and wrote it down. She said, "Never be afraid to trust an unknown future to a known God."[4] You can trust Him with the days ahead, for He has promised to guide you.

Seventh, He will satisfy your needs in a sun-scorched land and will strengthen your frame (v. 11). This is what Isaiah said earlier in chapter 30: "In quietness and confidence will be your strength." This is what he said in chapter 40: "Those who wait upon the Lord will renew their strength." This is what he said in Isaiah 41:10: "I am your God. I will help you, I will strengthen you, I will uphold you by My right hand of righteousness." This is the promise of personal strength, which is why it's at the heart of this book.

their translator. The area was tense because disaffected war veterans were angry with white farmers and landowners, one of whom lived behind gates near the school. As the Grahams returned from teaching and passed the farm, their truck was suddenly surrounded by about 120 enraged men who began chanting political slogans and shoving their vehicle from side to side.

Dorothy cried, "We're going to die."

"Well, if we're going to die," said Alan, "let's go out preaching the gospel." He jumped into the back of the truck and coaxed the unwilling translator to join him while Dorothy prayed in the cab.

Alan shouted to the mob, "I'm not here to talk about Mugabe or about the opposition," which further inflamed the throng. "But," he said, "I'm here to talk about Jesus, and if you'll shut up and sit down you might learn something.'"

In telling the story, Alan turned to me and said, "In a situation like that you've got to take authority, you see."

Alan gained their attention long enough to preach the gospel. He told them Jesus was the answer for Zimbabwe's problems and that Christ alone was the answer to their personal needs and problems. When he gave the invitation to receive Christ, twenty of the men indicated they wanted to receive Jesus as their Savior.

"I prayed with them and gave them New Testaments and booklets. Then I sent them home, and I said, 'If anyone else wants a booklet, come and I'll give you one.' The men got in a line and I gave out all my material. As I bent over to retrieve the last booklet for the last man, the leader stuck a gun in my neck and said, 'Pastor, it's time to go back to Harare [the capital].'"

"Take your gun away," said Alan. "I'm from Northern Ireland and guns don't really scare me. Why do you have a gun to my head?"

"We want you going back," said the soldier. "We don't want you staying here."

"Do you know what I do? I preach the gospel and help the poor."

"We know. That's why we're giving you a chance to go back to Harare."

Eighth, you'll be like a well-watered garden and like a spring wh
never fail (v. 11). Drive down the street during a drought and no
difference between gardens that have been irrigated and those dry.
Those who practice the right kind of faith will flourish, for they I
divine Gardener with ever-flowing, overflowing streams of rejuvena
and refreshment. He keeps us emotionally hydrated and healthy.

Ninth, we'll be given a special name—Repairer of Broken Walls (v. 12
As followers of Christ, we go by many names. Christians. Believers. The
Church. The Body of Christ. Disciples. Children of God. Saints. When I
was in college, we were called Jesus Freaks. But here in Isaiah 58, we have
one of the greatest titles we could ever wear. We are Repairers of Broken
Walls, of Broken Lives, of Broken Communities, of Broken Homes. God
will use us to reclaim and repair those who have broken down in life.

Finally, our lives will be flooded with joy (v. 14). We'll find our joy in the
Lord, and God will cause us to ride in triumph on the heights of the land
and feast on His inheritance (see v. 14).

These truths from Isaiah 58 are what motivated Alan and Dorothy
Graham. After confronting dire human suffering in Romania, Alan told
me, "I began reading in the Bible all God had to say about the poor and
helping the needy. I saw what Isaiah said in chapter 58 about the true fast.
It is to take care of the poor, and so Dorothy and I prayed about this and
God spoke very clearly to us about returning to Africa. We had been there
many years before. We hadn't been Christians at that time, and I became
an alcoholic there. My wife was going to divorce me, but then we turned to
Christ and He turned our lives around. Now, years later, we felt God's call
to Zimbabwe."

Alan and Dorothy secured a work permit, which in itself was a political
miracle, and they entered a nation gripped in racism and turmoil. The
country had descended into violence during the era of Robert Mugabe, and
things had gone from bad to worse. On the day I described earlier, Alan and
Dorothy traveled into the countryside to teach at school, accompanied by

The Grahams went back to Harare and learned the next day the remaining mob had murdered the nearby farmer after they left. But, undeterred, the Grahams went on helping the needy, feeding the poor, clothing the naked, providing school uniforms for children. They dug wells to provide water to communities. In one village they drilled a well and planned a day of dedication for the new water supply. A national pastor preached about the living water of Christ, and a thousand people received Jesus as Savior. "There's a church of a thousand there now," Alan told me.

A few years ago, Alan heard that in one community near Harare a sewer had become clogged and workers were sent to clear it. They found the bodies of twenty-five babies who had been thrown away, down the sewers.

"There's a lot of incest and rape in Zimbabwe among the poor," said Alan. "These little girls are having babies and they don't know what to do. That deeply disturbed me, and shortly afterward I stood up in a church in Napa Valley, California, where I was speaking, and told them I was going to open a home for abandoned babies in Harare."

Sitting in the audience, Dorothy was startled, and as soon as the service ended she said, "Alan! What are you doing? How are we going to start this with no money?"

Just then a lady tapped Alan's shoulder and asked, "How much will you need for that?" He said he had no idea, to which she replied, "I'll give the first $100,000 dollars to get it started."

That was the beginning of the Jabulani home for abandoned babies.[5]

"Isaiah 58 is a chapter I live by," Alan told me. "God will strengthen those who keep His true fast—helping the poor and wrapping the gospel in a sandwich for the hungry. As I do what God tells me, my life is changed, I become like a well-watered garden, the Lord strengthens my frame, uses me, and Jesus is glorified."[6]

We can't all move to Zimbabwe, but somewhere near you is a need you can meet, an orphan you can love, an elderly soul you can visit, a cause you can support, an empty stomach you can fill, or a disabled person you can assist. The Lord strengthens those who strengthen others. He will bless you. That's His way and His will now, just as much as it was 2,700 years ago when Isaiah recorded God's promise of the best kind of blessings for those with the right kind of fast and the right kind of faith.

> The LORD will guide you always; he will satisfy your needs in a sun-scorched land and will strengthen your frame. You will be like a well-watered garden, like a spring whose waters never fail. And you will be called, "The Repairer of Broken Down Lives."

A WORD FROM KATRINA

Just today I had an appointment with my neurologist. He was concerned about strengthening my frame. Sometimes when I've been out and about in my wheelchair, especially on Sundays, I come home almost bent over. I have a hard time sitting up. To be honest, I'm struggling with sitting upright even as I write this. So today my doctor prescribed a medication he hopes will strengthen my frame.

In Isaiah 58, the Lord gave us a prescription for strengthening our frames. His remedy is to focus on those less fortunate than ourselves. This is special to our family because several years ago our daughter and son-in-law adopted a little boy from overseas. Jude has a number of difficult issues, but how we love loving him!

Caring for Jude is a joy, but it's not our only obligation. One of my personal burdens is for the widows in our church. I can't do all I would like for them, but I'm learning ways to encourage them.

Perhaps you know someone with issues, someone needing special love. They may be in a wheelchair, battling a disability, discouraged, financially strapped, or lonely. The Lord strengthens our frames as we care for them.

EIGHT

Process Your Problems
and Arrive at Praise

The Sovereign Lord is my strength; he makes my feet like
the feet of a deer, he enables me to tread on the heights.

HABAKKUK 3:19

My friend Steven James is a gifted novelist and the author of thrillers. He's one of the best storytellers anywhere. Recently when we met for coffee he gave me a copy of a book he's published about the craft of writing fiction. Steven opened the book with an idea he calls the "Ceiling Fan Principle." Every autumn as students return to the classroom, he said, they're almost inevitably asked to write a little essay on the subject "What I did this summer." In Steven's view, this a boring exercise with a predictable set of answers.

"Well, a few years ago," Steven said, "I was visiting an elementary school while doing a residency on writing and storytelling. I arrived the day after spring break and told the students, 'Please, please, please do not tell me what you did over vacation. But can anyone tell me something that went wrong?'"

A fourth-grader raised his hand and said, "My cousin came over to my house, and we were having a contest to see who could jump the farthest off my bunk bed."

"What happened?"

"He went first and got pretty far, and I said, 'I can get farther than that!'"

"Well, what went wrong?"

The boy said, "I backed up to the wall to get a running start . . . and I jumped off the bed . . . and the ceiling fan was on. I got my head stuck in the ceiling fan, and it threw me against the wall—but I got farther!"

By that time, every student in the classroom was listening with real interest and some were rolling in the floor. Out of that experience, Steven developed what he calls his "Ceiling Fan Principle."

Here it is: you do not have a story until something goes wrong.

That's the first rule for good fiction—something has to go wrong. You don't have a story until something goes wrong.[1]

As I read that, I thought to myself—that's a pretty good rule for life too. That's the way it works with trusting the Lord. We don't understand faith until something goes wrong. Faith is a matter of relying on the Lord when our story encounters a problem. It's when we're caught in the ceiling fan. It's when we're slammed against a wall that we have to search out God's promises in the Bible and claim them by faith. Somehow our Christian faith works best when things go awry. And, of course, sometimes it seems everything is going awry.

That's what happened to Habakkuk, a prophet who lived 2,600 years ago in Judah. We know nothing about him from the historical books of the Old Testament; he isn't mentioned in the Bible outside his own little book. We know nothing of his family or the nature of his work. All we know about him is what we can glean from the three chapters making up the book bearing his name.

This book is a small jewel—a precious miniature. It's a very short volume and hard to find in the Bible. You might have to go to the table of contents to track it down; it's about two-thirds of the way through the Minor Prophets—the fifth book from the end of the Old Testament. But though the book of Habakkuk is small and hard to find, everyone who does find it and who studies it falls in love with it. It's a different kind of biblical literature. Habakkuk was a prophet and a preacher, but this is not a record of his sermons. It's an account of his struggles, a glimpse into his diary.

When you visit Isaiah, you hear a lot of preaching. When you read Ezekiel, you find a lot of visions. Most of the prophets were preachers who recorded their sermons in their books. But when we read Habakkuk, we don't encounter any sermons. It's more like a private journal. This is Habakkuk's own account of an emotional crisis he faced during the course of his ministry.

Sometimes during the course of our lives, we feel like we're having a breakdown of sorts. We're overwhelmed. Like you, I grow weary and worried. I have a hard time handling disappointment, and life is full of disappointing news. The world is turmoil-tossed, and we get caught up in it.

In Habakkuk's case, he became overwhelmed by the evil of his day and grew exasperated by what was happening around him. The conditions in his culture had deteriorated so much he didn't know if he could continue coping with everything confronting him. He didn't understand why God would allow things to get so bad. He didn't know how long he could keep up his courage. Habakkuk was tremendously confused and badly shaken, but he knew where to turn, and he scheduled an audience with the Lord to discuss his plight.

Perhaps you can identify with Habakkuk. I'm writing these words in the Northern Ireland home of my friends Philip and Denise, who have loaned me a bedroom and the use of Philip's study while on speaking engagements here. When Philip picked me up at the airport, I could tell his heart was heavy. He and Denise are pursuing an overseas adoption, and the process has taken a very discouraging turn. Having watched my daughter and son-in-law pursue an international adoption, I could understand a bit of what they're feeling, but their situation is particularly anguishing. I can tell they're working hard not to be overwhelmed by heartache, yet tears fill their eyes easily and often.[2]

Everyone has moments of heartbreak, and perhaps even now you feel overwhelmed. How easily and understandably we grow distressed in life—sometimes depressed and occasionally on the verge of collapse. We have to take time to collect ourselves. Like Habakkuk, we need a one-on-one with the Lord.

Habakkuk was a minor prophet with a major problem, and his small book teaches us how to process problems and arrive at praise. In the process, it provides the most visual description of faith in the Bible. Once you see its simple message, you'll never forget its lessons. Habakkuk shows us how to trudge through the valleys so we can tread on the heights.

The book of Habakkuk contains only three chapters; you can read it in just a few minutes. In the first two, Habakkuk records his conference with the Lord. It was a personal conversation. Habakkuk told the Lord his complaint and expressed his exasperation (Hab. 1:2–4). The Lord replied and gave a response (vv. 5–11). Habakkuk responded to God's answer by further stating his confusion (vv. 12–17), and God again gave him a fuller and more conclusive answer (2:2–20).

It was a simple two-way conversation: Habakkuk spoke, God spoke, Habakkuk spoke, God spoke. It was a back-and-forth counseling session. Then Habakkuk absorbed the information God gave, thought it through, adjusted his thinking, regained his perspective and his morale, and wrote a hymn (3:1–19). Chapters 1–2 reveal Habakkuk's struggle; and chapter 3 gives his song. In the first two chapters, he describes his confusion; in the last chapter, he states his conclusion.

This process works. From personal experience, I can tell you that problems are almost worth their stress when they drive us to open our Bibles, open our journals, open our hearts and minds, and open the door to our prayer closet. Like you, I've had many problems in life, but I've never faced one for which God hasn't given me a fresh perspective from His Word. If I can get into my Bible and find a verse from God, I can cling to that assurance until I arrive soundly on the other side of the situation.

PROCESSING PROBLEMS

Habakkuk began in verse 1 with these words: "The prophecy that Habakkuk the prophet *received*" (emphasis mine). This isn't a sermon he gave but a lesson he learned.

He then recorded his first complaint, beginning in verse 2 with the words "How long, Lord . . . ?" That's the essence of his cry. Habakkuk was sick and tired of the chaos around him. He didn't think he could stand it any longer.

> How long, LORD, must I call for help, but you do not listen? Or cry out
> to you, "Violence!" but you do not save? Why do you make me look at
> injustice? Why do you tolerate wrongdoing? Destruction and violence
> are before me; there is strife, and conflict abounds. Therefore the law is
> paralyzed, and justice never prevails. The wicked hem in the righteous,
> so that justice is perverted. (vv. 2–4)

Habakkuk was overwhelmed with the breakdown of morality and of law and order in his city. The nation of Judah was in steep decline. Habakkuk was trying to minister in a day when the foundations were collapsing. Imagine living in a land where law and order have broken down. That's occurring now in much of the world, though perhaps not yet in most Western nations. Our problem is the precipitous breakdown of the moral structure of our culture, which will sooner or later lead to a collapse of the framework of society. In some parts of the world, the full collapse—inwardly and outwardly—has occurred, and that's what Habakkuk was facing in his land.

As if that weren't enough, Habakkuk was facing personal internal confusion. It's terrible when, in the face of societal breakdowns, we absorb personal trials that test our strength. True for you now? Perhaps you don't know how long you can hang on. You feel like saying with Habakkuk, "How long do I have to put up with this situation? How long is this going to last?"

The Lord responded in verse 5: "Look at the nations and watch—and be utterly amazed. For I am going to do something in your days that you would not believe, even if you were told."

I've heard these words misinterpreted to give them a positive tone. "Just wait," someone will say. "Things look bad now, but God is about to do something so wonderful you wouldn't believe it if I told you."

But that wasn't the meaning God had in mind. He intended the opposite. Instead of giving Habakkuk encouragement, the Lord told him the bitter truth: Things are going to get worse—so much worse you wouldn't believe it if I told you. Your country is going to be invaded.

In prior chapters of this book, I've referred to the Babylonian invasion and the ensuing destruction of Judah. That catastrophic event also provides the backdrop for the book of Habakkuk. In verses 6–7, the Lord said:

> I am raising up the Babylonians, that ruthless and impetuous people, who sweep across the whole earth to seize dwellings not their own. They are a feared and dreaded people; they are a law to themselves.

The Lord went on to describe the coming Babylonian invasion of Israel. Habakkuk, remember, was already at the end of his rope. He was very discouraged with his society, and now God told him things would get worse. The pathetic prophet replied, "Lord, how long do I have to put up with this crumbling culture, with the decline and collapse of godliness in Judah?"

The Lord replied, in effect, "Not much longer. I'm about to do something you'll not believe. I'm going to let the Babylonians invade and destroy your land. I'm going to judge the city of Jerusalem and let her be swept away by the Babylonians."

If you want to know what the Babylonians were like, just think of ISIS. Things don't change much in the Middle East. Babylon's cruel, demonic, ruthless army swept from the Persian Gulf across Near Asia with the weapons of terror.

Understandably, the Lord's response further upset Habakkuk. Instead of making things better, this conversation made things worse. Habakkuk couldn't understand why God would allow Babylon to invade his nation and sweep away the Jews from Judah and Jerusalem. Things were bad in Judah all right; but the Babylonians were far worse than the Judeans. Habakkuk wanted to know how this made any sense.

He took up his end of the conversation again in verse 12: "LORD, are you not from everlasting? My God, my Holy One, you will never die."

He acknowledged God looks at things from the perspective of eternity, but we don't. Habakkuk yielded that point, but he continued, "You, LORD, have appointed . . . them to punish."

Read it like this: "Lord, You are eternal, You understand everything from an eternal perspective; and yet You have appointed *them* to punish *us*? We may be bad, but they are far *worse*."

He continued in verse 13:

> Your eyes are too pure to look on evil; you cannot tolerate wrongdoing.
> Why then do you tolerate the treacherous? Why are you silent while the
> wicked swallow up those more righteous than themselves?

We may have our problems, Habakkuk complained, but the Babylonians are viler than we. How is it right to use them in destroying us?

Habakkuk was grappling with the deepest questions we can ask. Why does God allow bad things to happen? Why does He allow bad things to happen *to us*? Why does life seem so unfair? Why do the wrong people sometimes win? Why are we sometimes abused by people far worse than we are?

Habakkuk finished his part of the conversation, and then, moving into chapter 2, he said: "I will stand at my watch and station myself on the ramparts; I will look to see what he will say to me" (v. 1).

It didn't take long. Look at the next verses in Habakkuk 2:2–3:

> Then the LORD replied: "Write down the revelation and make it plain on tablets so that a herald may run with it. For the revelation awaits an appointed time; it speaks of the end and will not prove false. Though it linger, wait for it; it will surely come and will not delay."

Translation: Write this down! Things will happen in sequence, and My divine plans will come to pass at the appointed time.

When life doesn't make sense we need to wait because it's all going to work out well for God's people in the end. Everything will work together for good to those who are God lovers, as we learn in Romans 8:28. The world is in process. The ultimate solutions are working their way through the pipeline at divine speed. In the final analysis, God is going to work out everything in conformity with the purpose of His will. He has a plan, and His plan is undeniable and irresistible.

What, then, do we do? We have to trust Him because those who please God must live by faith. Habakkuk 2:4 is a vital scripture for anyone needing strength for discouraging times: "See, the enemy is puffed up; his desires are not upright—but the righteous person will live by his faithfulness" or, as the margin puts it, "by faith." The just—those who please God—must live by faith. This is the key verse in the book of Habakkuk.

The famous third-century Jewish Rabbi Simlai analyzed the Old Testament and determined Moses had issued 613 different commands for his people to obey. In Psalm 15, David reduced the number by summarizing the commands into eleven statements. The prophet Micah boiled them down to three, which he posted in Micah 6:8. Isaiah reduced them to two in Isaiah 41:1. Then, according to Rabbi Simlai, the prophet Habakkuk recapped them all in one brief statement when he said "The just shall live by faith."[3]

This verse is so powerful and succinct it encapsulates the entirety of the New Testament. It summarizes the entire gospel. The New Testament writers quoted it three times—in Romans, Hebrews, and Galatians.[4]

There comes a time when all we can do is live by faith. We can't figure things out; we can't explain things; we can't solve or disentangle them; we can't clarify them or clear them up. We have no answers; we only have the Lord—and we have His great principle given to us fourfold in Scripture: "The just shall live by faith."

I can't tell you how many times I've calmed myself down by quoting Proverbs 3:5: "Trust in the LORD with all your heart." That verse doesn't provide all the answers, but it rests in Him who has all the answers. And I'd rather be in the hands of Him who has all the answers than to have all the answers in hand.

The Lord didn't stop the conversation at that point. He had a couple of other things to say. He went on in chapter 2 to tell Habakkuk the Babylonians would also be judged in due time; that all evil will one day be resolved; that everything wrong in the world will ultimately be righted; that every evildoer will be punished; and that, in the end, the earth will be filled with the knowledge of the Lord as the waters cover the sea.

Look at verses 13–14:

> Has not the LORD Almighty determined that the people's labor is only fuel for the fire, and the nations exhaust themselves for nothing? For the earth will be filled with the knowledge of the glory of the LORD as the waters cover the sea.

Here in one verse is God's ultimate plan for human history. This is a prophecy regarding the Millennium when Christ returns. The earth will one day be filled with the knowledge of the Lord as the waters cover the sea. But until then, what should our attitude be? Look at the last verse of the chapter—Habakkuk 2:20: "The LORD is in His holy temple; let all the earth be silent before him."

Just settle down. Don't panic. Don't give up. Be still, keep calm, and remember: The Lord is in His holy temple. He is on His heavenly throne. Let all the earth be silent before Him.

In Habakkuk 1 and 2, then, we have the personal record of a conversation between a confused soldier and his superior officer. Habakkuk said, "Lord, how long do I have to endure this?" The Lord replied, "Not much longer because things will get worse when the Babylonians arrive."

Habakkuk responded, "Lord, I know You see things from an eternal perspective, but this doesn't make sense to me. The Babylonians are worse than we are."

The Lord explained, "They too will be judged; but in the meantime I want you to trust Me, to live by faith. Let Me tell you the conclusion of everything: one day the earth will be filled with the knowledge of the Lord as the waters cover the sea. Until then, I am in My holy temple. Let all the earth keep silent before Me."

ARRIVING AT PRAISE

That brings us to Habakkuk's conclusion. After his confusion and after his conversation with the Lord, Habakkuk had a change of perspective. He processed his problems and arrived at praise. The burden of deep anxiety lifted from his heart. He took God at His Word and decided he would live by faith. He grabbed hold of God's long-term plan, and out of the experience he composed a song, a hymn, a psalm that is recorded in chapter 3.

This isn't unusual. In my series of books on the histories of our hymns—*Then Sings My Soul*—I discovered many of our great songs were penned out of catastrophic events and great suffering. For example, the thanksgiving hymn "Now Thank We All Our God" was written by Martin Rinkart following the anguish of the Thirty Years' War. The gospel song "It Is Well with My Soul," written by Horatio Spafford, came out of a personal tragedy. Luther Bridges wrote "He Keeps Me Singing" ("There's Within My Heart a Melody . . .") as he processed the grief of losing his wife and sons in a fire.

In that same spirit of "He Keeps Me Singing," Habakkuk wrote the hymn contained in his third chapter. Notice how Habakkuk 3 begins: "A prayer of Habakkuk the prophet. On shigionoth" (v. 1).

We're not sure what the word *shigionoth* meant, but it's generally considered a musical notation. It probably had to do with the tempo, and it identified this chapter as a hymn or a song. Notice too how the chapter ends in verse 19: "For the director of music. On my stringed instruments."

Chapter 3 begins and ends by letting us know this is a song of praise, a hymn, a spiritual song. It expresses musically the resolutions Habakkuk found in his heart. It represents his conclusion after his confusion.

The first half of the chapter is a vivid picture of how God comes to help His people. Verse 4 says, "His splendor was like the sunrise; rays flashed from his hand, where his power was hidden."

Verse 11–13 state: "Sun and moon stood still in the heavens at the glint of your flying arrows, at the lightning of your flashing spear. In wrath you strode through the earth and in anger you threshed the nations. You came out to deliver your people."

Then we come to verses 17–19, which arguably represents the most photographic depiction of faith within the covers of Scripture. This passage is so deep in its emotion and so simple in its expression that it's worth memorizing and keeping in our hearts. It brings the idea of *faith* down to where we live in the everyday world.

Though the fig tree does not bud and there are no grapes on the vines,

though the olive crop fails and the fields produce no food, though there

are no sheep in the pen and no cattle in the stalls, yet I will rejoice in the

LORD, I will be joyful in God my Savior. (vv. 17–18)

This passage tugs at my heart when I remember my father, John I. Morgan, who owned an apple orchard on the Tennessee and North Carolina border. It was a beautiful place—Sunset Orchard—and the Appalachian Trail ran right through it. Growing apples is hard work, and my dad labored week after week in anticipation of the fall harvest. But some years, a late freeze would kill the blossoms. I can still see the disappointment in his face when he realized the year would pass without any harvest in October. Yet he kept working, spraying, pruning, mowing, planting, and watching the sunset over Sunset Orchard, year after year.

It's hard to rejoice when the crops are killed, but we still have God's presence. We have His promises, His peace, His provisions, His protection, His providence working for our good, His personal care, and His ultimate paradise.

Habakkuk didn't say he was merely going to endure by faith. He said he would remain joyful, unsinkable in his attitude, happy in his heart. He had come to a place of realizing his joy shouldn't be based in his immediate situation but in his eternal Savior. Despite national calamity and personal adversity, Habakkuk was determined to see things from a different perspective and rejoice in the Lord.

Notice his last verse, Habakkuk 3:19, where we come to our key word—*strength*: "The Sovereign LORD is my strength; he makes my feet like the feet of a deer, he enables me to tread on the heights."

Eugene Peterson translates this "Counting on God's Rule to prevail, I take heart and gain strength. I run like a deer. I feel like I'm king of the mountain!"[5]

Only in the power of the cross can we go from dreading the hurts to treading the heights. Only through the power of the resurrection of Christ can we ascend the skies like eagles and traverse the mountains like deer. His sovereignty is our song, and we can rejoice in Him even when the trees produce no apples.

Not long ago, I spoke at the First Baptist Church of Houston, and the pastor, Gregg Matte, handed me a book he'd written on the subject of finding God's will. I read it with great profit. In one chapter, Gregg told of a terrible day in February 2006 when he and his wife, Kelly, had driven to the Texas Medical Center. They were subdued and sober on the trip. The radio was on, but they weren't listening to it. They were overcome with sorrow because the day before their dear preborn baby had passed away. The medical technicians had lost the heartbeat, and Kelly was going to have a procedure that would bring an end to what was no longer a living pregnancy. It was intensely, incredibly difficult; and Gregg and Kelly returned home, had a big cry, and started picking up the house and trying to stay occupied. Kelly's mother, Julie, was coming to help out for a few days, or so they thought. She actually had another reason for visiting.

Julie arrived, came in the door, hugged Kelly, and gave all the motherly comfort she could. But then she sat down and shared some news of her own. She had been diagnosed with cancer of the kidney, and her cancer was spreading.

Gregg was stunned and shaken, but as he watched Kelly, he saw in her a strength that amazed him. He wrote, "As we sat and talked in the living room, I was struck with the strength God was displaying through my wife. She had just lost a baby and was now conversing with her dying mother with kind, tender, understanding words. And she was shining with the love of Jesus Christ."

In the days following, Gregg wrote, Kelly sought God like never before. "You should see her Bible. It looks like it fell into the blender! Ink stained, pages curled, writing in every margin, cover torn. But the wear of her Bible also shows the protection of her heart. Imagine a woman losing a child, caring for her cancer-ridden mother and then speaking the eulogy at her mother's funeral. It was more than she could bear. But she trusted God to bear it for her, and He did. She leaned into Him and not away, and once again He proved Himself faithful."

In the middle of those harrowing experiences, Gregg credits Habakkuk 3:17–18 with giving both him and Kelly superhuman strength for the burdens: "Though the fig tree does not bud and there are no grapes on the vines, though the olive crop fails and the fields produce no food, though there are no sheep in the pen and no cattle in the stalls, yet I will rejoice in the LORD, I will be joyful in God my Savior."[6]

It was good enough for Habakkuk, Gregg told me, and it was good enough for them. Sometimes we have to say, "Everything else may go wrong, but the Lord never does. Everything else may fall to pieces—including me. But the Lord never does. He's still in His holy temple, and the just shall live by faith."

Once when I spoke on this subject to the workers of the Good News Rescue Mission in Indianapolis, the director, Dan Evans, told of a treasured song from his college days on this theme. The title was "Jesus Is the Lord of the Way I Feel." The words by Don Francisco paraphrased Habakkuk 3:17–19, and the chorus declared that Jesus Himself, not the circumstances, is the Lord of how we feel. He is our strength.[7]

There comes a time when our best strategy is drawing from His strength and living by utter faith. We can't figure out what the devil's going to do. We can't even explain what God is doing. We have no answers; we only have the Lord—and we have His great principle given to us fourfold in Scripture: the just shall live by faith.

Here, then, is the book of Habakkuk summarized:

Habakkuk said: "Lord, how long?"
I'm going to do something in your days . . .
"Lord, how come?"

Write this down and make it plain: The just shall live by faith. One day the earth will be filled with the knowledge of the Lord as the waters cover the sea . . . The Lord is in his holy temple; let all the earth keep silent before Him.

Then here's my song: "Though the fig tree does not bud and there are no grapes on the vines, though the olive crop fails and the fields produce no food; though there are no sheep in the pens and no cattle in the stalls, yet I will rejoice in the LORD, I will be joyful in God my Savior. The Sovereign LORD is my strength; he makes my feet like the feet of a deer, he enables me to tread on the heights" (Hab. 3:17–19).

A WORD FROM KATRINA

In drawing on God's strength amid disability, I'm often encouraged by the example of my mentor, Antoinette Johnson, who was unabashed in her witness for Christ. She was a Habakkuk 3 type of woman, and her memory influences me to this day. She didn't battle physical disability until she was older, but her life was full of challenges. She grew up wealthy and, before her conversion to Christ, was married several times to wealthy and prestigious men. When she committed her life to Christ, she was shunned and even made fun of. I witnessed the prejudice she bore, but she bore it with little concern.

She was an arduous Bible student. She was instrumental in opening a Christian student center in a castle (Schloss Mittersill) in Austria, and I was overjoyed to spend several months helping her renovate it for its grand opening.

I watched her faithfully pray in public in the restaurants and give out tracts. She opened a Christian bookstore in her dining room in Phipps Plaza in Palm Beach. I was her apprentice, and I watched as she found her strength in the Lord and treaded through her ministry with surefooted confidence in Him. Many of those rich people will answer to God for their treatment toward her, but others, I think, were brought to Christ through her witness.

Mrs. J—that's what I called her—made an indelible impression on me. She knew the Lord was totally in control, and she had no trouble doing His will in the strength He provided.

NINE

Strike a Missing Chord

Love the Lord your God with all your . . . strength.

Adelaide Procter loved poetry so much that in childhood she carried around a book of handwritten poems like other children dragged around toys. Her first published poem brought fame to her as a teen, and soon everyone was following her work, including Queen Victoria and Charles Dickens. After she became a Christian in her early twenties, she turned her talent to hymnody. She also began pouring herself into humanitarian and philanthropic work and, in the spirit of Isaiah 58, devoted enormous time, energy, and money to helping the homeless and downtrodden. She also crusaded for women's issues in Victorian England.

Adelaide worked so hard her health failed and she became bedridden in her thirties. At thirty-nine, she died of tuberculosis, and her death was considered a national calamity in England. But she left behind a body of poetry people are still reading 150 years later.

Adelaide's most famous poem is "The Lost Chord." Composer Arthur

Sullivan was so moved by reading it to his dying brother he set it to music, and it became the most famous song of the turn of the twentieth century. After the RMS *Titanic* went down, "The Lost Chord" was sung at a benefit concert for families of the victims. This was also the song Thomas Edison recorded to give an exhibition of the prototype of his new invention, the phonograph; and in the years since, a host of movies, television shows, and novels have based their plots around the mystery of the lost chord.

The poem tells of a woman who was weary and anxious. One night at twilight she sat at her organ as her fingers idly caressed the keys. She wasn't paying attention to the notes, but suddenly her fingers pressed a combination of keys that produced the most beautiful musical chord ever played.

It seemed to soar from the very soul of the organ. It was angelic. It was the touch of infinite calm. It brought instant harmony to the discordant feelings of life. It swept perplexity into perfect peace and carried worry away into worship. Then gradually the chord faded away and the mood was gone.

Try as she might, the woman was never able to remember which keys she had pressed or the notes she had played. It was a lost chord. Adelaide ended her poem by saying she longed to hear that chord again and *would* hear it again one day, but perhaps not till she got to heaven.

The reason this poem hits a chord with us, so to speak, is because most of us feel we're missing something. There's a lost chord somewhere, which, if we could only discover it, would make sense of life and sweep perplexity into peace. Something is missing in human society and in the human heart that would bring harmony to the discordant notes of our days.

What is it?

This is the deepest and most foundational question of philosophy. This question has dominated sermons, university lecterns, and the popular culture. Oprah Winfrey asked Paulo Coelho, the author of *The Alchemist*, about the one quality necessary to be a truly spiritual person. He told her the most important quality wasn't necessarily belief in God. Rather it was courage. "Courage is the first spiritual quality that you need to have," he said.[1]

The undergirding philosophy of the Olympic games is similar. At every opening of each Olympiad, the athletes recite the Olympic creed, which was adapted from a speech given at the 1908 Olympics by Episcopal bishop Ethelbert Talbot. It says: "The most important thing in the Olympic Games is not to win but to take part, just as the most important thing in life is not the triumph but the struggle. The essential thing is not to have conquered but to have fought well."[2]

The actress Audrey Hepburn said, "The most important thing is to enjoy your life—to be happy—that's all that matters."[3]

Entertainer Taylor Swift said, "I think it's the most important thing in life to dance to the beat of your own drum and to look like you're having more fun than the people who look cool, like they fit in."[4]

All that sounds good to postmodern humanity, but what answer would I give if asked about life's ultimate purpose? I've offered a variety of opinions about this in sermons over the years. Knowing God, I said at one point, is the most important thing. Worshipping Him is the most important. Evangelizing the nations is the most important thing we can do. Being happy in Christ is the best thing. I often quote the opening of the Westminster Shorter Catechism, which says, "Man's chief end is to glorify God, and to enjoy Him forever."

All those are variations of the same theme, and they're not wrong. Yet as I studied for this book, I saw something more clearly than ever. It's true we need courage. It's true evangelism and worship are all-consuming priorities and that worship is the missing jewel of the church. It's true Paul said his determined purpose was knowing God. And, yes, our chief end is to glorify God and enjoy Him forever.

But how would Jesus answer the question about life's ultimate priority? If you asked Christ about the greatest thing in life, what would He say? What is the apex of it all? The missing chord? The first and greatest commandment?

LOVING GOD IS THE MOST
IMPORTANT THING WE DO

We aren't left to figure it out ourselves. In Deuteronomy 6, there's a passage of Scripture called the Shema from the Hebrew word meaning "hear." It says: "Hear, O Israel: The LORD our God, the LORD is one. Love the LORD your God with all your heart and with all your soul and with all your strength" (vv. 4–5).

Centuries later when Jesus was treading the hills and hovels of Palestine, someone asked Him to name the greatest thing we can ever do. What is the first and greatest commandment? In three parallel passages in the Gospels, Jesus quoted the Shema. He said, "Love the Lord your God with all your heart and with all your soul and with all your mind. This is the first and greatest commandment." (Matt. 22:37–38).

Again He said, "Love the Lord your God with all your heart and with all your soul and with all your mind and with all your strength (Mark 12:29–30). This, He said, is more important than anything else. It's the greatest thing in the world.

What does it mean to do something with all your strength? When was the last time you or I did something requiring all our strength? Sometimes at a major sporting competition, we may see athletes compete with all their strength, breaking records and putting every last ounce of effort into their events. Sometimes they win the gold or the silver or the bronze medal; but it's even better when their award has a little designation beside it—the letters PR, which stand for Personal Record. That means the athlete not only beat everyone else in that particular event, but also his or her own record. That athlete ran or swam faster than he or she had ever done before.

To do something with all our strength implies intensity, sustained effort, and ongoing concentration. That's the way we're to love God—and it's the most important thing we can do. Until studying for this book, I'd never looked at it quite like this. I've known these verses. I've sung the hymns and songs about loving Jesus. But I view this subject in a deeper way now than previously, though I still feel in the kindergarten stage of it.

What helped me was looking up every occurrence of the word "love" in the Bible. When I sorted them out, I found tons of references about loving other people and a galaxy of verses about how God loves us. But amid the references, I found about fifty passages specifically about loving God. Working through them, I realized I've underestimated the importance of this. It's not that I haven't known about loving God, but until I went through the passages one by one, I'd never noticed how important it is to love our Lord with all our strength.

We're made to love God. In the garden of Eden, God came down and visited Adam and Eve. He loved them and they loved Him, and that was the normal state of things. The most terrible thing about sin is how it strips away the natural love we should have for the Lord. The apostle Paul characterized the last days as being a time when people will be lovers of pleasure more than lovers of God (2 Tim. 3:4). In fact, the simplest definition of idolatry is loving something or someone more than we love the Lord.

The apostle Paul put it dramatically in 1 Corinthians 16:22, when he said "If anyone does not love the Lord, let that person be cursed!" The old Aramaic expression is *anathema*. It means to be damned and cut off from the Lord.

If I were to ask about the worst sin it's possible to commit, you might say child abuse or genocide or some other horrendous act. But the worst sin of all—the fountainhead of all the others—is the failure to be in love with God. The worst sin, logically, is the breaking of the greatest commandment. If we can determine the greatest commandment, we can identify the worst sin. Jesus said the first and greatest commandment is loving God.

THE LORD MEASURES OUR LOVE FOR HIM

I also noticed as I studied these fifty passages on loving God that, in a way I can't fully understand, God measures our love for Him. He's always probing to see whether we love Him as we should. There's an interesting paragraph about this in Deuteronomy 13:1–3, when Moses warned the Israelites:

> If a prophet, or one who foretells by dreams, appears among you and announces to you a sign or wonder, and if the sign or wonder spoken of takes place, and the prophet says, "Let us follow other gods" (gods you have not known) "and let us worship them," you must not listen to the words of that prophet or dreamer. The LORD your God is testing you to find out whether you love him with all your heart and with all your soul.

If there comes into your life an influential or special person who impresses you but tends to draw you away from the Lord, it may be a test to see if you really love the Lord with all your strength.

In a similar way at the end of John 21, the risen Christ appeared to the apostle Peter and asked him a series of question—or actually the same question three times—corresponding to the three times Peter had previously denied Christ: "Do you love me more than these?" He asked. "Do you love me? Do you love me?" (vv. 15–17).

The Bible says, "Peter was hurt because Jesus asked him the third time, 'Do you love me?' He said, 'Lord, you know all things; you know that I love you'" (John 21:17).

If the risen Christ suddenly appeared in your kitchen or in the front seat of your car, and if He were going to ask you one question, what would it be? It might be about the most important ultimatum in life. He might look at you, look around at your habits or environment or priorities, and tenderly ask, "Do you really love Me?"

LOVING THE LORD MEANS LOVING
SOMEONE CURRENTLY INVISIBLE

Jesus, having ascended to heaven, probably isn't going to visibly appear to you, but to Peter the question is eternally valid. In his first epistle, he told us loving Jesus means we are loving someone currently invisible. When Jesus appeared to him on the shores of Galilee in John 21, Peter overtly saw our Lord and audibly heard His voice. But then Jesus ascended to heaven and disappeared into the clouds of glory. In writing to his friends afterward, Peter said, "Though you have not seen him, you love him; and even though you do not see him now, you believe in him and are filled with an inexpressible and glorious joy" (1 Peter 1:8).

Is it possible to love someone who's currently invisible to you? Of course; it's the most natural thing in the world. When my son-in-law, Ethan, was in Iraq with the armed forces, we didn't love him any less, but more. I'm writing this while away from home, but I don't love my wife any less, but more. When my parents passed away and went to heaven, I didn't stop loving them. I can't literally see their faces now or hear their voices. But I love them more now than I did while they were alive. I'm eager to see them again.

What fickle, foolish people we'd be if we only loved those in our immediate presence. Jesus came to earth, lived for us, died for us, rose for us, ascended to heaven for us, and is preparing a place for us. He will come for us. Loving Him isn't mystical or magical or imaginary. It's the most rational and natural thing in the world.

LOVING THE LORD MEANS WE CAN
HARDLY WAIT FOR HIS RETURN

Among the Bible's fifty passages about loving God, there's also an emphasis on the anticipation of His return. Because we love Him, we can hardly wait to see Him. The apostle Paul, looking forward to his own death and the Lord's return, wrote, "Finally, there is laid up for me the crown of righteousness, which the Lord, the righteous Judge, will give to me on that Day, and not to me only but also *to all who have loved His appearing*" (2 Tim. 4:8 NKJV, emphasis mine).

Over the past few years we've seen videos on television of men and women in the armed forces who have returned home and surprised their loved ones. A little girl at school turns around, and there's her dad. A boy opens a big box under the Christmas tree, and out pops his dad. When we're away from those we love, we long for the time when we'll see them again. We long for a reunion. I believe the Lord placed the clouds in the sky and gave us beautiful sunrises and sunsets to remind us of His return. The last prayer of the Bible is "Even so, come, Lord Jesus." We can tell how much we love Jesus by determining how excited we are about soon seeing Him.

UNTIL HE COMES, WE'RE TO DEMONSTRATE OUR LOVE FOR HIM

As I studied the biblical passages about loving the Lord, I noticed how demonstrative the verses were. Someone recently told me, "My dad was not a demonstrative man. He loved me, but he wasn't very expressive of that love." Well, we're all different. But God is demonstrative toward us—Romans 5:8 says, "God demonstrates his own love for us . . ."—and He longs for us to respond in kind.

How do we, then, demonstrate our love for Him? I went through these passages looking for the answer to that question, and I found eight ways.

First, by putting Him before everything and everyone else in life. Jesus said in Matthew 10:37: "Anyone who loves their father or mother more than me is not worthy of me; anyone who loves their son or daughter more than me is not worthy of me. Whoever does not take up their cross and follow me is not worthy of me."

That's a verse worth thinking about. I can't tell you how much I love my daughters. You can say the same for your loved ones. When something goes wrong in their lives, it bothers us worse than something going wrong in our own lives.

Yet Jesus said we should love Him more than we love our sons or daughters or parents or children or even our very lives. How can He expect something like that? Because He knows that when He's in first place, all our other relationships will be healthier for it. When we love Him above all, we'll have all His love from above flowing through us to our sons and daughters and fathers and mothers. We'll have His resources of love, joy, peace, patience, and kindness to pour into all the relationships of our lives.

Helen Roseveare wrote, "To love the Lord my God with all my soul will involve a spiritual cost. . . . To love the Lord my God with all my mind will involve an intellectual cost. . . . To love the Lord my God with all my strength will involve a physical cost. I must give Him my body to indwell, and through which to speak, whether He chooses health or sickness, by strength or weakness, and trust Him utterly with the outcome."[5]

Second, by saying we love Him. All of us know the three most important words in any marriage: "I love you." Many of us can remember the first time we said those words to the person who would become our life partner. I recently read of a man who was a tremendous athlete. He won awards and was presented trophies before thousands of people. But he could never really enjoy the accolades because the one thing he most needed was missing—a proud father who would say to him, "Son, I love you."

The Bible tells us if we love the Lord, we'll tell Him. Psalm 18:1 says, "I love you, LORD, my strength."

When did you last tell the Lord something like this? "I love You, Lord. I love You with all my heart, soul, strength, and mind. I love You more than father or mother, more than son or daughter. I love You with an imperfect love for I'm an imperfect person; but nevertheless, I love You, O Lord, my strength, and I love You with all my strength."

Third, by acknowledging His name. Psalm 91:14 says, "'Because he loves me,' says the LORD, 'I will rescue him; I will protect him, for he acknowledges my name.'"

I grew up singing the little chorus "I have decided to follow Jesus." Reportedly this hymn came from the nation of India and has it roots in an incident in the mid-1800s. A Welsh missionary had won a man to the Lord in the state of Assam. The man was saved along with his family. Persecution quickly ensued, and the village chief demanded the convert to renounce his faith. But the man replied, "I have decided to follow Jesus." Amid continuing threats, he said, "Though no one joins me, still I will follow." The man and his wife were executed, but their witness later led to the conversion of many in their town. Some years later, the Indian evangelist Sadhu Sundar Singh put the words to music.

The Bible says that if we love God we'll be eager to be known by His name. We will gladly and proudly acknowledge Him before others. We'll be eager to say, "I have decided to follow Jesus."

Fourth, by loving His Word. The longest chapter in the Bible—Psalm 119—is full of this emphasis.

- *I delight in your commands because I love them*—verse 47
- *Oh, how I love your law! I meditate on it all day long*—verse 97
- *I hate double-minded people, but I love your law*—verse 113
- *I love your statutes*—verse 119
- *I love your commands more than gold*—verse 127
- *Your promises have been thoroughly tested, and your servant loves them*—verse 140
- *See how I love your precepts*—verse 159
- *I hate and detest falsehood but I love your law*—verse 163
- *Great peace have those who love your law, and nothing can make them stumble*—verse 165
- *I obey your statutes, for I love them greatly*—verse 167

My father bought me a little New Testament from a traveling evangelist when I was young, and then, when I was older, he bought me a study Bible. I can recall very few days in my life when I haven't read God's Word. I love it cover to cover, don't you?

When I read the book of Genesis, I discover the Maker of the universe, the roots of my history, and the basis for all my relationships. In Exodus, I begin to understand the wonder of redemption. When I read the books of the Law, I begin to see what God is like in His moral character and what He expects of me in morality and ethics. When I read Joshua and Judges and the historical books of the Old Testament, I learn about the providence of a God who was forging a nation as a channel through which His redemption would touch the world with a coming Messiah.

When I read the book of Job, I know how to respond to sorrow. When I read the book of Psalms, I learn how to worship. When I read Proverbs, I know how to control my tongue and my temper.

When I read Isaiah, I see a Suffering Savior, who tells me how to mount up with wings as eagles, how to walk and not grow weary, and how to run and not be faint.

When I come to the Gospels, I stand amazed in the presence of Jesus the Nazarene, and I ask in wonderment, "What manner of man is this that even the winds and the waves obey Him?" When I stand at the foot of Calvary, I see my sin and my Savior. Then I turn the page, and I'm in resurrection garden at the moment Christ bursts from the tomb, saying, "Because I live, you will live also."

Coming to the book of Acts, I'm caught up in the adventure of taking the gospel to the globe, and I find passion and purpose for life. I proceed to Romans and learn what it means to be justified by grace through faith alone, and on to Ephesians where I study a catalog of my riches in Christ, and on to Philippians where I can rejoice in the Lord always.

The letters of John give me a new commandment but it's still the old one—to love God and others. Jude tells me to contend earnestly for the faith once for all delivered to the saints. And when I come to the final book of the Bible, I have a panorama of God's revelation of the future, and I end my journey in the New Heavens and the New Earth. Coming to the last promise of the Bible, I hear Him say, "I am coming quickly." And before closing the covers, I echo the last prayer of the Bible: "Even so, come, Lord Jesus."

This book is a lamp unto our feet and a light unto our pathway, and we love it dearly because we love its Author.

Fifth, by obeying Him. Jesus said, "If you love me, keep my commands. . . . Whoever has my commands and keeps them is the one who loves me" (John 14:15, 21). The first epistle of John says, "This is how we know that we love the children of God: by loving God and carrying out his commands. In fact, this is love for God: to keep his commands. And his commands are not burdensome" (1 John 5:2–3).

Sixth, by hating evil. The Bible says, "Let those who love the LORD hate evil" (Ps. 97:10). We hate it in the world, and we hate it within us, and our hatred helps us fight it and fend it off.

Seventh, by conversing with Him in prayer. Psalm 116 says, "I love the LORD, for he heard my voice; he heard my cry for mercy. Because he turned his ear to me, I will call on him as long as I live" (vv. 1–2).

Eighth, by helping God's people. The apostle John said, "Whoever claims to love God yet hates a brother or sister is a liar. For whoever does not love their brother and sister, whom they have seen, cannot love God, whom they have not seen. And he has given us this command: Anyone who loves God must also love their brother and sister. . . . Everyone who loves the father loves His child as well" (1 John 4:20–5:1).

For many years, Carl J. Printz was Norway's Consul to Canada. When he was ninety-nine years old, he was interviewed on television. The journalist asked him, "Give us the rule you have followed during your long and useful life, the rule which has most influenced your life and molded your character." Printz replied, "I would mention one definite rule—one must be temperate in all things." Then he paused and added, "Perhaps I should say temperate in all things except one—fulfilling the commandment to love God with all your heart, soul, and mind and your neighbor as yourself. These are the only things we can rightly do with excess."[6]

He's right. We can't love God too much, but we can love Him better. Our love for Him can grow richer. Our adoration and devotion to Him can deepen. And our daily walk with Him can yield more loving fellowship from day to day.

HOW GOD BLESSES THOSE WHO LOVE HIM

There's a final category of verses to observe. Out of the fifty passages on loving God, several of them represent promises from God to those who love Him. I tried to categorize these verses but I finally gave up. There aren't enough categories, so I'll just list them in the order they appear in the Bible. Don't skip over the following list; make them a personal Bible study. Look up each one and claim the specific blessings God has for those who love Him.

When we love God with all our strength:

- He will show love to us for a thousand generations—Exodus 20:4–6
- He will send rain in its season and drive out the enemy—Deuteronomy 11:13–15
- He will become our very life and bestow tangible blessings on us—Deuteronomy 30:19–20
- He will make us like the sun rising in its strength—Judges 5:31
- He will turn to us and have mercy on us—Psalm 119:132
- He will watch over us—Psalm 145:17–20
- He will love us and make His home with us—John 14:21, 23
- He will work all things for our good—Romans 8:28
- He will prepare for us things that are beyond what our eyes have seen, what our ears have heard, and what our minds have imagined—1 Corinthians 2:9

- He will give us all the grace we need—Ephesians 6:24
- He will bestow on us the crown of life—James 1:12
- He will confer the kingdom He has promised—James 2:5

But these things don't explain *why* we love Him. The real motivation for our love is simple—we love Him because He first loved us (1 John 4:19).

Several years ago, I spent two lovely days in Assisi, Italy, wandering around and thinking about Saint Francis, the medieval friar. Here's the way he was described by a biography I picked up while there: "Those who knew Francis told he was always occupied with Jesus. Jesus he carried in his heart, Jesus in his mouth, Jesus in his eyes, Jesus in his hands, Jesus in all his members. Often he forgot where he was and what he was doing at the thought of Jesus, and with such glowing love was he moved toward Jesus Christ, yes, and with such intimate love did his Beloved reply, that it seemed to the servant of God himself that he felt his Savior almost continually before his eyes."[7]

You might feel Francis was a bit obsessive. But contrast that with the members of the church of Ephesus in Revelation 2:4 who had drifted away from their "first love."

Let's stick with Francis.

After all, if we're going to be obsessive about something, shouldn't it be the greatest thing in the world? If we're going to journey through life with a song in our hearts, shouldn't we strike the missing chord?

Love the Lord your God with all your heart and with all your
soul and with all your mind and with all your strength.

A WORD FROM KATRINA

In 1968, I moved from Maine to Florida to work for Antoinette Johnson; but later, after her bookstore ran into difficulties, I found a job with the

Palm Beach County School Board. Then I transferred to the City Clerk's Office of the City of West Palm Beach. This was the job I'd been waiting for because it provided a good income for Florida's Gold Coast. I attended a Bible church in North Palm Beach and sat under the ministry of Dr. C. Ernest Tatham, and during those years I began the practice of daily morning devotions. That's when I really began learning what it meant to love the Lord my God with all my strength.

I needed God's strength because my job was very demanding. I managed the records for the city of West Palm Beach and the minutes of the commission meetings. This job had to be done accurately and daily. No computers—just shorthand tablets, an electric typewriter, and metal filing cabinets.

That was years ago, but I've never outgrown the lessons I learned in those days. Now as a pastor's wife who struggles with disability, I'm no longer able to take shorthand, use keyboards very easily, or file things away in cabinets. But I have more time than ever to sit at my desk, study God's Word, pray, and cultivate my communion with Him.

What a privilege!

TEN

Galvanize Yourself Against Discouragement

[Abraham] did not waver through unbelief
regarding the promise of God, but was
strengthened in his faith and gave glory to God.

ROMANS 4:20

I have a letter in my files from a friend named Judy, who endured a grim period of discouragement several years ago. Her melancholy was triggered by a mean-spirited letter from a friend, which sent her morale into hibernation for the winter. But it wasn't just a damaged friendship that cast her down; Judy also had marital problems, and she was overwhelmed. At the same time she was trying to teach the Bible to high school students.

After a long and dark January, February arrived and with it came Valentine's Day. Judy hoped for a box of chocolates and a long-stemmed rose from her husband, not because of the gifts themselves but because she needed the reassurance of his love. But no gifts were forthcoming.

She was in bleak spirits the next day as she prepared the Sunday lesson for her teenagers. The subject had to do with the biblical names for God, and that week the focus was on the title *El Roi*, which means "the God who sees me." This phrase was used in the Bible by Hagar, the troubled mother of Ishmael, in Genesis 16:13. But as Judy thought about this, she melted down and lashed out at the Lord in anger.

"If an earthly father saw his child hurting like I am," she complained in prayer, "he would do something to help her. You're supposed to be El Roi, the God who sees, and not only the God who sees, but the God who knows beforehand all that happens. You're supposed to provide in advance all that's needed." With a broken heart, she anguished before the Lord over a husband who didn't care enough to give her a rose or a box of chocolates.

Finishing her outburst, Judy wiped her eyes and remembered she needed to move the clothes from the washer to the dryer. As she passed the back door, she had a strange feeling she should open it and look outside. She found a bag hanging on the doorknob. The word *LOGOS* was printed on the bag and inside was a Valentine's card that talked about the God who sees and watches over us. Accompanying the card was a Christian book of reassurance—with the picture of a long-stemmed red rose on the cover. Something else was in the bag too—a small box of imported chocolates.

There in the kitchen, as Judy told me in her letter, she fell on her knees and asked God's forgiveness for doubting His love and care. "He truly showed Himself to be El Roi to me that day," she said, "and in my mind I somehow pictured a Bible with the pages turning from one to the next, and a hand stamping the word *TRUE* on each page."[1]

Judy's story provided me with a great definition of faith. Faith is picturing the word *TRUE* stamped on every page of the Bible, inscribed across every promise, imprinted on every verse, and engraved on every word. Faith is the act of galvanizing ourselves with God's truth against discouragement, even when friendships falter, marital woes accumulate, and no one arrives with long-stemmed roses. More than galvanizing our hearts, faith is gold-plating our souls with the promises of Scripture.

Put differently, faith is keeping up our spirits when things aren't going well. It's remaining calm when things heat up. It's facing the circumstances knowing Him who is above the circumstances and focusing on His promises when we're tempted to fret over the problems. It's staying reasonably cheerful whether the tide is in or out because the shifting of the tides matters little to the Rock of Gibraltar. Even storms don't disturb His serene solidarity, for He is our Rock. He is El Roi, the God who sees us.

I like thinking of faith in visual terms like that, and one of my hobbies is locating scriptural descriptions of faith in the Bible.

For example, in the gospel of John, a royal official approached Jesus with a desperate plea. The man asked Jesus to come heal his boy. "Sir," the official said, "come down before my child dies." But Jesus had His own agenda and didn't do as the man asked. Instead He said, "Go, your son will live." John 4:50 says, "The man took Jesus at his word and departed." The story ends on a happy note, for as the man was still on his way, his servants met him with news the boy had recovered. When the official inquired as to the time his son got better, they told him, "Yesterday, at one in the afternoon." The Bible says, "Then the father realized that this was the exact time at which Jesus had said to him, 'Your son will live'" (John 4:43–54).

Try to put yourself in the shoes of that father. His son was near death, and he didn't want to leave the boy's bedside; yet he knew the only hope was in the Healer of Galilee. So he made the hardest decision of his life, leaving his fevered child and traveling day and night to the Great Physician. Jesus, however, told him to return home because his son would recover.

What would you do? Would you feel great disappointment or great relief? It depends on your faith in Jesus. The Bible says, "The man took Jesus at His word."

I'm not sure there's a better definition or depiction of faith in the Bible. Faith is simply taking Jesus at his word.

But let me suggest another definition. In Acts 27, the apostle Paul was aboard a ship teeming with terrified sailors—276 people in all. A terrific storm had lashed the ship day after day until all hope was gone. Even the seasoned seamen had given up. Everyone was cold, drenched to the skin, with stomachs empty and minds numb; they clung to handholds as the ship rose and fell among mountainous troughs and swells. The ship groaned and creaked like a house about to collapse.

That's when Paul rose and shouted over the wind with an astounding message: "Last night an angel of the God to whom I belong and whom I serve stood beside me and said, 'Do not be afraid, Paul. You must stand trial before Caesar; and God has graciously given you the lives of all who sail with you.' So keep up your courage, men, for I have faith in God that it will happen just as he told me" (Acts 27:23–25).

There's another golden definition of faith—keeping up our courage because we know everything will happen just as God has told us.

When you begin looking for them, you'll find a lot of ways faith is expressed in the Bible. For example, Psalm 86:11 says, "Teach me your way, LORD, that I may rely on your faithfulness." What is faith? It's relying on God's faithfulness. The apostle Paul used a similar phrase in 2 Corinthians 1:9: "This happened that we might not rely on ourselves but on God, who raises the dead." Faith is relying not on ourselves but on God who raises the dead. Faith is . . .

- Taking God at His Word,
- Knowing things will happen as He has said,
- Relying on the faithfulness of Him who raises the dead,
- "Confidence in what we hope for and assurance about what we do not see" (Heb. 11:1).

Let's add one more biblical depiction: faith is being fully persuaded God has the power to do what He has promised. That description is found in Romans 4:21 in the story of the Old Testament Patriarch Abraham.

SAVING FAITH

The passage in Romans 4 has its primary application in what I call *saving* faith—that is, the simple act of trusting Jesus to reconcile us to God, who gives eternal life and saves us from sin, death, and hell. Whenever we dip into the book of Romans, it gives us a chance to remind ourselves of the wonderful theme of justification, which means being restored to an intimate friendship with God by the forgiveness of sin and the gift of righteousness that comes through the Calvary-work of Jesus Christ. Romans is the greatest explanation in human literature of what it means to reconnect with the God who created us.

The first three chapters of Romans describe how damaged and hopeless we are. These chapters tell us, in effect, we're like a person who has fallen into a deep hole, into a narrow shaft descending hundreds of miles beneath the surface of the earth. It's a bottomless pit and we can never climb out. With great effort we may lift ourselves an inch or two, maybe a foot. We may be able to climb up the walls a few yards, but then we fall back. We can never see the sunlight. We are trapped and perishing in our own sins.

But Romans 3:21–31 turns on the light and describes how God reached His hand down to us—a nail-pierced hand. He declares, "All have sinned and fall short of the glory of God, and all are justified freely by his grace through the redemption that came by Christ Jesus. God presented Christ as a sacrifice of atonement, through the shedding of his blood—to be received by faith" (Rom. 3:23–25).

We are justified by God's grace through the simple and normal process of faith, of trusting Christ to save us.

Turning the page to chapter 4, Paul said this is how God worked in the Old Testament, even before Christ died on the cross. Justification by grace isn't a new doctrine. It's not something Paul invented. Those who walked with God in the Old Testament also did so on the basis of faith.

Paul's "Exhibit A" is Abraham, founder of the Jewish race. Romans 4:1–3 says:

What then shall we say that Abraham, our forefather according to the flesh, discovered in this matter? If, in fact, Abraham was justified by works, he had something to boast about—but not before God. What does Scripture say? "Abraham believed God, and it was credited to him as righteousness."

This is a reference to Genesis 15 and the story of the Abrahamic Covenant. God said to Abraham in the days of Genesis, "Do not be afraid . . . I am your shield, your very great reward" (v. 1). God indicated Abraham would have children and grandchildren and a line of descendancy that would eventually bring redemption to the world through a coming Messiah. Abraham was a hundred years old at the time, and his wife Sarah was aged, so the prospects were humanly impossible. But God took Abraham outside into the night and directed his attention to the twinkling stars. "So shall your offspring be," said the Lord (v. 5). Genesis 15:6 says, "Abram believed the LORD, and he credited it to him as righteousness."

Abraham was declared righteous in God's sight at that moment on the basis of faith alone. This was before the Law was given. This was before the Jewish sign of the covenant was given. This was before Calvary. But God had promised a plan of redemption, Abraham believed it, and on the basis of faith he was declared righteous.

People in the Old Testament were saved on the basis of their faith in what God *was going to do* when Jesus died on the cross, just as we are saved by faith in what Christ *did* on the cross. In every epoch and era, among every tribe and tongue since the fall of humanity, there has only been one means of reconnecting with our Creator—by grace through faith in our Lord Jesus Christ.

That is saving faith. We can never make it to heaven by our own efforts. We can't climb out of the holes of hopelessness. We can't live lives good enough. But we can place our faith in what Christ did when He died and rose again; and as we confess Him as Lord and believe in our hearts that God raised Him from the dead, we are saved (see Rom. 10:9–10).

In my book *Every Child, Every Nation, Every Day,* I tell how a friend of mine, Czeslaw Bassara of Poland, exercised saving faith. As a young man Czeslaw became the leader of the Communist organization in school. Returning home late one night, he heard his mother praying for him: "Dear God, save my boy and get him out of this way of living."

"Stop praying!" Czeslaw shouted. "I will never become a Christian! I choose Communism as my way of life!"

Soon afterward, Czeslaw's father invited the local church to meet in their house. Enraged by the thought of Christians worshipping in his very room, Czeslaw built a homemade bomb and placed it in the cellar beneath this bedroom. He detonated it during the observance of the Lord's Supper. The blast damaged the house and rattled the nerves of the worshippers, but no one was killed. The church responded by praying earnestly for the young Communist.

A few months later, Czeslaw was invited to a Christian camp six hundred kilometers from his home in Gdansk. He decided to go, though he later confessed he didn't know why. Night after night he sat through the presentation of the gospel, and it began to grip his heart. One night, when invitation was given, he went forward—not to be saved but to try to understand how the Christians wielded so much influence over young people. An old Polish preacher explained the message of Jesus to the responders, and many were saved. In the silence of the moment, the young Communist seemed to hear the Lord telling him: "This is your time. It will never again be given to you." At that moment, Czeslaw opened his heart and trusted Christ as his Savior.

He returned home and began attending the church he had bombed. Soon he was invited to teach children. He enrolled in theological studies and went on to devote his life to the work of Child Evangelism Fellowship in Europe.[2]

This is saving faith—and it's strong enough to change your life forever.

SUSTAINING FAITH

Being delivered from sin and receiving the gift of eternal life is something that happens to us once for all; but the principle of faith is ongoing and life-long. It's something we practice from that point until we arrive in heaven. The Christian life is described as walking by faith, not by sight (2 Cor. 5:7). Just as we need faith for eternal salvation, we need faith for daily living. When we trust Christ as our Savior, we're entering a faith-based life. Just as we depend on God's promise of salvation to take us to heaven, we rely on all His other promises to sustain us along the way. Faith is the victory that overcomes the world (1 John 5:4).

Thus the story of Abraham continues. Though he trusted God in Genesis 15, the promises made to him were not instantly fulfilled. It took a long time for Abraham and Sarah to bear the promised son. But Abraham kept up his courage, he took the Lord at His word, he believed it would be just as God told him, and he was fully persuaded God had the power to do what He had promised.

That brings us to Romans 4:19–21:

> Without weakening in his faith, he faced the fact that his body was as good as dead—since he was about a hundred years old—and that Sarah's womb was also dead. Yet he did not waver through unbelief regarding the promise of God, but was strengthened in his faith and gave glory to God, being fully persuaded that God had power to do what he had promised.

As Christians, we can be weak in our faith or we can be strengthened in our faith. When we're weak in our faith, we're weak in every other way. We're weak in our inner resolve. We're weak in our ability to handle stresses and strains. We're weak in our emotions and attitudes. We're weak in our witness and testimony.

But when we are strong in our faith, we are strong in all those areas.

How, then, do we go through life without weakening in our faith but being strengthened in our faith instead? This passage gives us the answers.

First, faith is trusting in a trustworthy God. Our faith is only as good as the object in which it's placed. This is the most basic rule of faith I've discovered. Last summer, I was hiking along an old set of abandoned narrow-gauge railroad tracks in the mountains near our family home in East Tennessee. I came to a bridge over a gorge, an old railroad bridge. The wood was rotten and the metal rusted. It wasn't safe to walk across, much less drive a train across.

Were I an engineer, I might have all the faith in the world in that bridge despite its appearance. I could have said, "I believe that bridge will hold up this train." But the train wouldn't have survived the passage. On the other hand, if I were driving a train across a sturdy new bridge, I might have a weak faith and even be nervous; but the train would make it just fine. The important thing about faith isn't its size but its object.

When it comes to life, we have to consider the object of our faith. In verse 17, Paul said Abraham placed his faith in "the God who gives life to the dead and calls into being things that were not."

Two aspects of God's power are described. First, He gives life to the dead. If you discard the reality of God, you're left with no other viable explanation for life in our universe. It didn't just spark into being out of non-existence. It didn't just come about by strange, random, purposeless, accidental sets of electrical or chemical reactions. It came from the eternal God. And the God who created life can re-create life; that is, He can raise the dead with Exhibit A being the resurrection of Jesus Christ from the grave on Easter Sunday. He can deliver on His promise of everlasting life. If God can do that, He is worth trusting. He is worthy of our faith.

Second, God is the one who calls into being things that were not. This is creation. God can create from nothing, *ex nihilo*. I recently had an amazing conversation with a Chinese gentleman who now lives in Canada. His name is Xinwei Lin. He grew up in southeast China and was educated in biology and neuroendocrine science. He completed his PhD in 1991 and became a university professor in China. He came to the United States in 1993 and moved to Canada to do post-doctorate work in biomedical science. He was very involved in researching and teaching evolutional theories. But he and his wife met a group of Christians, and in the course of time Xinwei was wonderfully saved. He and his wife were baptized on the same day. Xinwei enrolled in seminary, completed his studies, and today serves as senior pastor of a Chinese-speaking church in Canada.

"What happened to your evolutionary beliefs?" I asked him.

"I was saved with the heart, not with the head," said Xinwei. "But once I became a Christian everything made sense intellectually. I looked at the same scientific facts, I looked at the same evidence, I looked at the same research, and they made perfect sense from the perspective of creation and within a creation-paradigm."

He gave me an example. He had been very involved in research on goldfish because goldfish have a remarkable brain system that, in some ways, resembles that of humans. If you are evolutionist, you say, "Aha! Goldfish and humans descended from the same evolutional line." But if are a creationist, you say, "Aha! God used a similar design in the brain structures of these two different creatures." Similarities do not imply descendancy. A gilder may resemble an eagle, but that doesn't mean they share a common line of organic descent.

This brilliant scientist, upon becoming a Christian, recognized that everything he knew about science fit the framework of a scriptural worldview. We have a God who raises the dead and who brings into being things that are not. Our faith isn't in our faith but in our God.

Second, faith is trusting God via His promises. God communicates His blessings to us through specific promises recorded in His Word. His first set of promises has to do with our eternal life, our salvation and forgiveness of sins—all the aspects related to justification. But those promises represent the gateway into an entire life that's sustained in every way and on every day by the multitudinous promises of God. Notice how the word "promise" occurs in this passage in Romans 4:

- *Abraham and his offspring received the **promise** . . . —verse 13*
- *The **promise** comes by faith—verse 16*
- *He [Abraham] did not waver through unbelief regarding the **promise** of God, but was strengthened in his faith, and gave glory to God, being fully persuaded that God had power to do what He had **promised**—*verses 20–21

That final phrase is the best definition of faith I've found in the Bible. Faith is being fully persuaded God has the power to do what He has promised. As we hit rough times, we need to focus our minds on the specific promises God gives to meet our needs. There have been many nights when I couldn't have slept had I not forcibly focused my mind on certain promises God has given me in His Word.

Dr. Ted Rendall is a brilliant man with a photographic memory. He reads a complete book every day, and he's been doing that all his life. His personal library contains 32,000 volumes, and he can tell you pretty much what all those books say. Last year, Dr. Rendall told me of a tragedy he endured years ago.

He was born and raised in Edinburgh, Scotland, and moved to Canada as a young man. Shortly after arriving in North America, he received word his father had drowned at sea. The news came in the form of a telegram from his brother. Dr. Rendall's father had been employed aboard a merchant ship, sailing between Dundee and Edinburgh with a load of sand. The vessel was caught in a storm and somehow the coverings or the hatches must have blown off in the storm. The rain was so torrential it soaked the sand and the ship sank. There were two lifeboats, and some of the men were able to crowd into the lifeboats. But in the violence of the storm, one of the lifeboats overturned, resulting in more loss of life.

When news came, Dr. Rendall was devastated. He was far away and there was nothing he could do. There were no goodbyes. He was away from family and friends, and he had to carry on despite grief. "But," he said, "God sustained me. He gave me sustaining grace through a specific verse of Scripture—Psalm 71:16."

Dr. Rendall didn't quote the verse to me, so I returned to my room and looked it up. It said: "I will go in the strength of the Lord GOD; I will make mention of Your righteousness, of Yours only." By focusing his thoughts on that verse, Dr. Rendall drew strength from the Lord.

That was Ted Rendall's experience, and it can be ours. We stand on the same promises.

The psalmist said, "The LORD is trustworthy in all he promises and faithful in all he does" (Ps. 145:13). Peter said, "His divine power has given us everything we need . . . he has given us his very great and precious promises" (2 Peter 1:3–4). Paul wrote, "For no matter how many promises God has made, they are 'Yes' in Christ. And so through him the 'Amen' is spoken by us to the glory of God" (2 Cor. 1:20).

Faith is *not* positive feelings based on hopeful hunches. It is firm reliance in unbreakable promises made by an unchangeable God, inscribed in His Word, purchased by the blood, and ratified by the resurrection of Jesus.

We are strengthened in our faith as we're increasingly persuaded—fully persuaded—that God has the power to do what He has promised even if, at the moment, the tide of circumstances is flowing in the opposite direction.

Faith means trusting God in every age and stage in life. Abraham first heard the voice of God when he lived in Ur of the Chaldeans, and we see his life unfold in undulating stages from Genesis 11 to Genesis 25, when he died at age 175. But his epitaph is recorded in Hebrews 11:17: "By faith Abraham . . . embraced the promises."

It pays to study the promises God has issued throughout Scripture so we can recall and embrace them as needed. This habit meant everything to Abraham, and it means everything to us. One night a couple of weeks ago,

I felt a little tremor of panic. The deadline for this book was near, and I had back-to-back trips, work obligations, and family concerns. I wondered if I could relax enough to go to sleep. Then Psalm 121 came to mind: "I will lift up my eyes unto the hills from whence comes my help. My help comes from the LORD who made heaven and earth."[3]

I went to bed and visualized a set of lofty mountains reaching to heaven and envisioned invisible rays of help coming in my direction. The next morning as I led the pastoral prayer at church, I found myself quoting Psalm 121, and every word strengthened me. The next day I visited a man in the hospital. He was sitting up, but extremely weak. I knelt beside him and quoted Psalm 121 word for word; then I went back and repeated the beginning: "I will lift up my eyes unto the hills from whence comes my help. My help comes from the LORD, who made heaven and earth." He nodded with understanding. That evening he died, but I can still see the affirming look in his eyes as I quoted those words.

As I write this, I'm at Liberty University, where I've taught six sessions in two days, and tonight my mind is spinning, but it's still spinning around Psalm 121. I feel like Charles Spurgeon, who said in a sermon: "One word of God is like a piece of gold, and the Christian is the gold-beater, and he can hammer that promise out for whole weeks. I can say myself, I have lived on one promise for weeks, and want no other. I want just simply to hammer that promise out into gold leaf, and plate my whole existence with joy from it."[4]

That's a great analogy because the psalmist said God's words are "more precious than gold, than much pure gold" (Ps. 19:10). Gold leaf is solid gold that's been hammered into thin sheets to cover a surface such as wood, stone, or metal—a process called gilding. If you've ever been in a gilded palace, you know how dazzling it is.

Go for gold. Adopt the gold standard. Let's hammer the promises of El Roi—the God who sees us—into a gold plate for our souls as we travel toward the Golden City, not wavering or faltering through unbelief but being strengthened in faith, giving glory to God, and being fully persuaded God has the power to do what He has promised.

We may not live to be as old as Abraham, but as long as we're on earth, let's emulate his faith. "By faith he made his home in the promised land like a stranger in a foreign country . . . for he was looking forward to the city with foundations, whose architect and builder is God" (Heb. 11:9–10). When you do the same, you'll galvanize yourself against discouragement.

A WORD FROM KATRINA

Paul encouraged his readers to study the example of Abraham; he was reminding them of their heritage. We often draw strength by recalling the heritage God gives us. I'm often encouraged, for example, by remembering my mother, Hilja Lyyli Polvinen. She grew up in rural Maine, the daughter of Finnish immigrants, and her father led her to Christ after he was saved in a local revival meeting.

Mom grew up in a large, hard-working farming family—I recall old pictures of the fields with horses and hay. After graduating from nursing school in Portland, she married my dad, Walter. He was a woodsman and mechanic, and she worked in the hospital. She was one of the nurses who attended me when I had surgery at age nine.

Mom had determined strength. We were a large family, and she cooked a lot and was well-known for her nisu, a Finnish coffee bread. I can still smell the cardamom seed. We would stop morning and afternoon for coffee, and sometimes in the evenings; it was tradition, coffee being the national drink of Finland.

Mom was a strong and unflappable Christian. She sang in Finnish in the Finnish-speaking Congregational Church in our little town of West Paris, Maine. Later I fondly recall her accompanying me to New York City for a job interview at the Waldorf-Astoria, and I was hired because my soon-to-be-boss, Antoinette Johnson, loved my mother.

When I was a young mother and preacher's wife trying to do it all, she advised me to get on a schedule. I did, and it saved my life. She's been in heaven many years now, but her example still strengthens me like Abraham's did for the original readers of Romans.

ELEVEN

Live Like the Rich Person You Are

I pray that out of his glorious riches he may strengthen
you with power through his Spirit in your inner being.

EPHESIANS 3:16

I'm enough of an introvert to dread social occasions, yet I try to be as conversational as possible. A couple of years ago when I spoke at a blue ribbon event for wealthy people, I felt out of my league. Though they were some of the most gracious people I've met, rich people, I observed, live and think a bit differently. At the gala supper, for example, the man on my left said something about returning home the next day and getting back to work. "Yes," I said naively, "my plane leaves tomorrow at noon. When does yours leave?"

"Whenever I tell it," the man replied without the slightest trace of presumption. I went blank, nibbled at my food, and turned to the woman on my right. I made a comment about the wonderful meal, which somehow led to a discussion of her home kitchen, which, she said, was her favorite room. I thought I'd get some conversational mileage out of recipes, so I asked what she enjoyed cooking. "Oh, I don't cook," she said with a warm smile. "I have a cook." I silently prayed for the program to begin.

These were humble and good-hearted people attending a conference where they would contribute large sums to worthy causes. They listened appreciatively as I taught leadership and stewardship principles, and I enjoyed being with them. But I realized they lived differently than I do.

Returning home, I saw a report in *Slate* magazine about billionaires. There are 2,325 of them in the world, holding over $7 trillion or four percent of the world's total wealth. About a hundred live in New York City and another 85 in Moscow. Europe has more billionaires than any other continent. The average net worth of each of these men—they are nearly all men—is $3.1 billion, and the average age is sixty-two. Most of them have four homes worth about $94 million.[1]

But the magazine omitted one fact. The humblest child of God has a larger portfolio than the richest person on earth. I checked the footnotes on the *Slate* article, and the writer didn't consult the book of Ephesians, which tells us, in effect, that every Christian is wealthier than all 2,325 billionaires put together.

When you think of the richest people on earth, think *you*. Think those who know and love Christ. Think of being heirs of God and co-heirs with Christ of incalculable riches. Think of His billions of blessings, and try imagining the billions of years we'll enjoy them.

This is the theme of Ephesians.

Ephesians has six chapters, which divide into two sections. Chapters 1–3 describe how rich we are in Christ, and chapters 4–6 tells us how we should then live, for rich people live differently than others.

If you want to see how this unfolds through the epistle, read the first three chapters and underline each reference to riches, wealth, inheritance, and so forth. You'll come across phrases like these: "blessed . . . in the heavenly realms with every spiritual blessing in Christ . . . his glorious grace, which he has freely given us . . . in accordance with the riches of God's grace that he lavished on us . . . you were marked in him with a seal, the promised Holy Spirit, who is a deposit guaranteeing our inheritance . . . the riches of his glorious inheritance . . . .God, who is rich in mercy . . . the incomparable riches of his grace . . . heirs . . . the boundless riches of Christ . . . his glorious riches."

Coming to the end of this section, the apostle Paul burst into a prayer as lofty as any in the Bible. It's one of the Bible's great strength passages, as well as one of our great 3:16s—Ephesians 3:16. He prayed the Ephesians would realize how rich and strong they were:

> I pray that out of his glorious riches he may strengthen you with power through his Spirit in your inner being.

I confess I'm overwhelmed with this verse and its context. I can't do it justice. It would take weeks to unpack it all.

Some of the best comments I've read on this passage came from the pen of Arthur T. Pierson, who lived over a hundred years ago and had uncanny insights into Scripture. He called Ephesians the "Switzerland of the New Testament." It unveils a series of Alpine heights, he said, and as we read this letter we rise from one elevation to another until we have wondrous views of God's grace toward us both now and forever.

I like this analogy because last year I had the opportunity of speaking to the International Baptist Convention in Interlaken, Switzerland. A friend and I flew into Milan and drove over the high passes in the Alps. We stopped at every overlook, overwhelmed with the vistas. That's how I feel whenever I study Ephesians.

The summit, according to Pierson, is Ephesians 3:14–21, the Mont Blanc of Scripture. There we go above the snake line, over the timberline, beyond the mists and clouds, into the vistas of the heavenlies.[2]

In the original Greek, Paul wrote these verses in one long, unbroken burst—a run-on sentence, as we say. It's as though he were too excited to stop for breath. Modern translations break the passages into sentences for clarity, but Paul wrote it in one mad dash, not pausing for breaks.

Imagine driving through this passage like a wide-eyed traveler, winding upward and onward into high elevations of truth. We can drink in the view by pulling over at seven overlooks as they occur in text.

GOD STRENGTHENS US WITH POWER THROUGH HIS SPIRIT

The first panorama occurs in Ephesians 3:16. The passage begins with a prayer for God to strengthen us with power through His Spirit. The word *power* is the Greek word *dynamis*, which is where we get our English words *dynamite* and *dynamic*. This term occurs over and over in the New Testament—119 times—and it's translated by several English words: *power, might, strength, ability, authority*. It refers to the omnipotence of the eternal God, conveyed to us by the Holy Spirit in a way that strengthens us to do whatever God assigns or allows each day. We could transliterate it as *dynamism*. It means divine and dynamic energy. Note how the New Testament writers used this word:

- The dynamism of God is what saves us. Romans 1:16 says: *I am not ashamed of the gospel, because it is the **power** of God that brings salvation to everyone who believes.*
- The dynamism of God empowers our witness. Jesus said: *You will receive **power** when the Holy Spirit comes on you; and you will be my witnesses* (Acts 1:8).
- The dynamism of God makes us overflow with joy and peace. Romans 15:13 says: *May the God of hope fill you with all joy and peace as you trust in him, so that you may overflow with hope by the **power** of the Holy Spirit.*

- The dynamism of God is what enables us to make an impact on the world, as we read in 2 Corinthians 4:7: *We have this treasure in jars of clay to show that this all-surpassing **power** is from God and not from us.*

- The dynamism of God gives us confidence for whatever comes in life, for 2 Timothy 1:7 says: *For the Spirit of God does not make us timid, but gives us **power**, love and self-discipline.*

- The dynamism of God is what provides everything we need. Simon Peter wrote: *His divine **power** has given us everything we need for a godly life through our knowledge of him who called us by his own glory and goodness* (2 Peter 1:3).

- The dynamism of God keeps us going when we're attacked by adversity. Paul wrote in 2 Corinthians 12:9: *My grace is sufficient for you, for my **power** is made perfect in weakness.*

- The dynamism of God keeps us fresh and flourishing in our work for the Lord. Colossians 1:10–11 says we're to bear *fruit in every good work, growing in the knowledge of God, being strengthened with all **power** according to his glorious might so that you may have great endurance and patience.*

- The dynamism of God is nothing less than the personal power of Jesus Christ conveyed into our lives by the Holy Spirit. The apostle Paul said about his ministry: *To this end I strenuously contend with all the energy Christ so **powerfully** works in me* (Col. 1:29).

You can see how the Lord loves this word *power*, and notice how often these references point to the power of God through Christ, energizing us by means of the Holy Spirit.

Wade C. Graber, a Baptist pastor, said that years ago he was in school, driving fifty-eight miles round-trip every day for his classes. He was getting up early and going to bed late, and he was also employed on a part-time basis. One morning, he said, during his time alone with God, his tired eyes read Ephesians 3:16. "The instant I finished reading this verse, I experienced an 'infusion.' It was electrical . . . I was immediately empowered, energized, and invigorated by the indwelling Spirit." Many years have passed since then, but Graber wrote, "I continue to quote Ephesians 3:16 on multiple occasions. The electric physical sensation is not always experienced, but the strengthening ministry of the Spirit still occurs in my times of need."[3]

HE STRENGTHENS US OUT OF HIS GLORIOUS RICHES

We don't travel far into the text before the next panorama. God strengthens us out of His glorious riches. When I was a child, I read comic books like Richie Rich and Scrooge McDuck, and often the colorful pictures showed great vaults teeming with gold coins and precious metals. Sometimes the cartoon characters dove into their stash of gold coins like a swimmer plunging into a pool. In today's real world, a few places boast almost cartoonish amounts of wealth. Look at pictures of Dubai and Abu Dhabi, for example, with their incredible six-star hotels, fabulous resorts, world-class architecture, and man-made islands, all financed by vast oil reserves. Visit a home like the Biltmore Estate or the Hearst Castle and imagine living there.

When Christ followers think of their wealth, they don't see cartoon characters, desert sheikhs, or American tycoons. They see heaven-bound people who enjoy:

- A relationship with God we could never earn.
- Constant access we could never buy to a throne that will never fail.
- Purpose in life we could never purchase.
- Precious promises no amount of money could acquire.
- A Book that surpasses silver and gold.
- A wisdom that exceeds diamonds and rubies.

- A personal Guide who leads our steps and turns everything for our good.
- A peace that transcends understanding.
- A love that surpasses knowledge.
- An eternal home described as mansions laid up for us in heaven, occupying real estate in a celestial city whose builder and maker is God, with golden streets, translucent buildings, open gates, a crystal river, and angelic neighbors.

To the biblical writers, this was worthy of their worship. Paul began Ephesians by saying, "Praise be to the God and Father of our Lord Jesus Christ, who has blessed us in the heavenly realms with every spiritual blessing in Christ" (Eph. 1:3).

Peter began his first epistle on a similar note: "Praise be to the God and Father of our Lord Jesus Christ! In his great mercy he has given us new birth into a living hope through the resurrection of Jesus Christ from the dead, and into an inheritance that can never perish, spoil, or fade. This inheritance is kept in heaven for you" (1 Peter 1:3–4).

Songwriters have celebrated these eternal assets for years with stanzas like

> My Father is rich in houses and lands;
> He holdeth the wealth of the world in His hands!
> Of rubies and diamonds, of silver and gold,
> His coffers are full, He has riches untold.[4]

And I'm a child of the King, adopted into His family "through Jesus Christ, in accordance with his pleasure and will—to the praise of His glorious grace" (Eph. 1:5–6). He allots strength out of these boundless riches. The Phillips translation of Ephesians 3:16 says: "I pray that out of the glorious richness of His resources He will enable you to know the strength of the Spirit's inner reinforcement."

HE STRENGTHENS US IN OUR INNER BEING

That brings us to our third overlook: He strengthens us in our inner being. "I pray that out of his glorious riches he may strengthen you with power through his Spirit in your inner being" (Eph. 3:16).

What is our inner being? I've puzzled about that. There's a heart and center to almost everything God has made. Take the earth for example. Scientists tell us our planet has an inner core of nickel and iron, but it's mysterious because no one has ever journeyed to the center of the earth, not even Jules Verne. The solar system also has a center around which everything orbits, and it's the sun. In the same way, the tiny atom has a dense nucleus around which the electrons orbit. Even apples have cores, bones have marrow, and trees have an inner circle around which the rings grow. There are concepts of centers and coils in mathematics related to the golden mean and Fibonacci spiral. God specializes in creating center points in the created order.

In the same way, you have a center—a soul, as repeatedly affirmed in Scripture.

- *People look at the outward appearance, but the LORD looks at the **heart**,* says 1 Samuel 16:7.
- Psalm 103:1 says, *Praise the LORD, my **soul**; all my **inmost being**, praise his holy name.*
- Likewise, Psalm 139 says, *You created my **inmost being**. . . . Search me, God, and know my **heart*** (vv. 13, 23).
- Second Corinthians 4:16 says, *Though our outer self is wasting away, our **inner self** is being renewed day by day.*[5]
- Hebrews 4:12 says, *For the word of God is living and active, sharper than any two-edged sword, piercing to the division of **soul and of spirit**.*[6]
- First Thessalonians 5:23 says, *May your whole **spirit** and **soul** and body be kept blameless at the coming of our Lord Jesus Christ.*

- The apostle Peter had something to say about this too. In 1 Peter 3:3–4 he wrote, *Your beauty should not come from outward adornment . . . Rather it should be that of your **inner self**, the unfading beauty of **a gentle and quiet spirit**, which is of great worth in God's sight.*

We are more than chemicals, more than bodies that perish, more than random mutations. We have an inner personality made in God's image, an inner self, an inmost being, which is eternal. In Jesus Christ, the Holy Spirit enters our spirit and strengthens us in our inner dimensions. Far from human eye or personal observations, down in the deep places of life, you have a source of inner strength. This is where God strengthens you and enables you to be a stronger father or mother or husband or wife or witness or evangelist. We can take advantage of this strength by consistently offering Ephesians 3:16 as a personal plea to God: "I pray that out of Your glorious riches You will strengthen me with power through Your Spirit in my inner being."

HE STRENGTHENS US SO CHRIST WILL DWELL IN OUR HEARTS THROUGH FAITH

Why do we need such inner strengthening? That's the next stop on the tour. It's so Christ can dwell in our hearts through faith. The passage goes on to say: "I pray that out of his glorious riches he may strengthen you with power through his Spirit in your inner being, so that Christ may dwell in your hearts through faith" (Eph. 3:16–17).

I don't think this verse is talking about the initial act of inviting Christ into our hearts and lives. The word "dwell" here involves long-term habitation. The idea is asking Christ to settle down and truly make Himself at home as the Owner of the house, as it were. *The Living Bible* says, "I pray that Christ will be more and more at home in your hearts, living within you as you trust in Him."

Jesus lives in the hearts of His children, but He may not always feel at home there. Imagine moving in with someone only to encounter things that distress you. Imagine being uncomfortable with conditions under your own roof. Perhaps that's true for you now. You're living in an apartment, condo, or house, but you're not happy with your environment. Now imagine Jesus feeling that way when He dwells in your heart and life.

As His Spirit strengthens our souls, we'll increasingly grow more like Him. He'll be more at home in our hearts. He'll increasingly be the host and not the guest—the Lord of the lair. His personality and passions will gradually clean out all the closets, cupboards, and crannies of our minds. He's a good housekeeper and homemaker, and He likes to discard filth before it accumulates. Jesus will settle down and dwell within us with happiness and holiness.

Ephesians 1:7 declares we have forgiveness of sins according to the riches of God's grace, but Ephesians 3:16 goes further: He grants us inner strength out of His glorious riches. How we need both!

HE STRENGTHENS US TO COMPREHEND HIS LOVE

That leads us to the fifth elevation: as we're strengthened with power in our inner being and Christ dwells in our hearts, He enables us to comprehend His love.

I pray that out of his glorious riches he may strengthen you with power through his Spirit in your inner being, so that Christ may dwell in your hearts through faith. And I pray that you, being rooted and established in love, may have power, together with all the Lord's holy people, to grasp how wide and long and high and deep is the love of Christ, and to know this love that surpasses knowledge. (Eph. 3:16–19)

In the passage, Paul described God's love in geometric terms. In his comments on Ephesians 3, Dr. A. T. Pierson pointed out: "He treats the love of God as a cube, having breadth and length, depth and height. The cube in the Bible is a perfect square, and from every angle it presents the same appearance. Turn it over, and it is still a cube—just as high, deep, and broad as it was before."

The Holy of Holies in the Old Testament tabernacle was in the shape of a perfect cube, as was the Holy of Holies in the Jerusalem temple. In the book of Revelation, the celestial city is described as being as long and deep as it is high. The city of New Jerusalem has the dimensions of a perfect cube.

Pierson then went on to describe these various sides of the love of God—how wide and long and high and deep it is.

- How *wide* is the love of God? It's as wide as the outstretched arms of Christ on the cross, wide enough to take everybody in, broad enough to reach you.
- How *long* is the love of God? He loves us with an everlasting love. There never was a time when God did not love you; and there will never be a time when He does not love you. His love reaches from everlasting to everlasting; it spans the two eternities, past and future.
- How *high* is the love of God? It's higher than the highest star. It's as high as the highest heaven; as high as the highest throne. It lifts us up to heaven, and it lifts us up to God.
- How *deep* is the love of God? It's deeper than all our problems and pain; deeper than all our distresses and disasters. It's deep enough to reach down into the depths of all our sin and our grief and pluck us out.[7]

HE STRENGTHENS US TO BE
FILLED WITH HIS FULLNESS

That leads to the next elevation: He strengthens us so we'll be filled with His fullness:

> And I pray that you, being rooted and established in love, may have power, together with all the Lord's holy people, to grasp how wide and long and high and deep is the love of Christ, and to know this love that surpasses knowledge—that you may be filled with the measure of all the fullness of God. (Eph. 3:17–19)

I cannot tell you what that phrase means—"hat you may be filled with the measure of all the fullness of God." I just know the Bible talks a lot about being filled with various aspects of God and His ways. We're to be full of faith, full of goodness, full of joy, full of the Spirit. I think it's best summed up in an old hymn:

> *Oh, fill me with Thy fullness, Lord,*
> *Until my very heart overflow;*
> *In kindling thought and glowing word,*
> *Thy love to tell, Thy praise to show.*[8]

As I prepared this message I thought of a conversation I had with Mrs. Hester Rendall, who had been on the Hebrides Islands with the noted preacher Duncan Campbell. This was in the 1950s shortly after a period of revival had swept over the islands, especially the Isle of Lewis. The revival had occurred between 1949 and 1952, and Hester was there in 1958; but the afterglow was still evident.

One evening Hester went to a church service where a sense of the presence of the Lord came down so strongly that the people prayed earnestly and hardly dared to lift their heads. After awhile, her friend said they should probably go home and go to bed. Hester said, "Why? We've only been here a few minutes." The friend said, "It's three o'clock in the morning."

God is nearer than we know, stronger than we realize, more loving than we can imagine. Being filled with the measure of all the fullness of God must involve energy, enthusiasm, and reinvigoration.

As I talked about these things with the Rendalls that day, my imagination went to work. I saw a great ventilation shaft like a tremendous vertical duct reaching from heaven to earth and from the celestial city right into our hearts. Here on earth, the air is poisonous. The atmosphere is toxic. But God pumps the atmosphere of heaven into the innermost spirits of His people as they trust in Him, and the oxygen of heaven revives and strengthens us. We are filled with His wind, with His breath, and with His Spirit.

Even if revival doesn't sweep across our nation or our world, we have a constant source of fresh air for our souls, filling us with the Spirit and with the pure, fresh, energizing, invigorating, rejuvenating, restoring, revitalizing breezes of heaven, direct from God and siphoned into our inner beings.

Just as our lungs are filled with strengthening air, so we're to be inwardly filled with all the strengthening fullness of an omnipotent God. We are filled with the measure of all the fullness of God.

To grow in this experience, I suggest making the book of Ephesians a lifelong study. You can read all six chapters in about ten minutes, and as you read it repeatedly, its message will indelibly register on your mind and heart. You'll be richer with every reading.

Consider memorizing Ephesians 3:16 or perhaps even the entire passage (vv. 14–21). Offer it often as prayer for yourself. Do as Paul did—pray it for others. There's no more powerful prayer in the Bible for your husband, wife, children, grandkids, pastor, friend, or fellow worker. Pray in faith, believing God is able to exceedingly, abundantly answer.

TO HIM BE GLORY FOREVER

And don't forget the last two verses of the chapter—the seventh elevation, the pinnacle, the highest point of the passage, and the ultimate view: "Now to him who is able to do immeasurably more than all we ask or imagine, according to his power that is at work within us, to him be glory in the church and in Christ Jesus throughout all generations, for ever and ever! Amen" (Eph. 3:20–21).

These verses are summits of divine truth, but they're as practical as everyday life. While I was in Switzerland last year, I asked my friend Roy Harrison, who lives there, if he recalled a time when he was strengthened with power by the Holy Spirit in his inner being as described in Ephesians 3. Yes, he told me, many such times. He recalled a specific incident in the 1980s when Poland was still under Communism. Roy had agreed to travel there and clandestinely teach a course in leadership, but the class was underground and the location was secret.

In something evocative of the Cold War, Roy was told to fly from Zurich to Warsaw, where someone would quietly meet him and put him in a train to Bielsko-Biala, where he would again be met and taken to the hidden location. But everything went wrong when Roy missed his flight. Yet somehow, through odd coincidences and sheer determination, he found his way to Bielsko-Biala, where a taxi driver, who could only speak Polish, improbably took Roy to the very house near the village of Djengelow, where the students were meeting. Roy arrived just in time to gather his notes and step to the lectern for his first class.

"That was a very stressful situation," Roy said. "To make matters worse, I drank impure water and became sick. But at every point, I felt God's strengthening presence in my inner being and the end result was a powerful week with believers behind the Iron Curtain."[9]

Those who know Christ are the richest people on earth and the strongest. The Lord isn't worried about our financial wealth or physical strength.

It's the Spirit's inner reinforcement we most need, and it's not for our glory but for His.

> Now to him who is able to do immeasurably more than all we ask or imagine, according to his power that is at work within us, to him be glory in the church and in Christ Jesus throughout all generations, for ever and ever! Amen. (Eph. 3:20–21)

A WORD FROM KATRINA

One of my caregivers is a single mom working at Vanderbilt while getting her nursing degree and doing business in creative design. She never gets enough sleep, and she travels all over the county in her pursuits. Yet she takes care of me with a ready smile and strength in her inner being. Her young daughter is a graceful participant as well.

When I quizzed her about her upbeat attitude, Schyler testified to me she has learned to just throw things on the Lord. She said, "I see everything—I'm a nurse."

She can't afford to get bogged down emotionally in her life because her daughter needs a steady home life as much as possible. And she is providing it. I am so blessed to have such a strong young woman helping me—and I can help her by asking God to continually strengthen her with all power by His Spirit in her inner being.

TWELVE

Learn to Rejoice Whatever, Whenever, Wherever

I can do all this through him who gives me strength.

PHILIPPIANS 4:13

T wo aged men—Prisoner A and Prisoner B—sat in adjoining cells amid the squalor of a brutal penitentiary. Both old revolutionaries had been captured in different locations, fighting for different causes. Neither had known the other until now. They were chained like animals, and their surroundings were wretched. There was no climate control in this prison—no heat or air-conditioning. Depending on the time of year, prisoners would freeze or fry. There was no electricity. No electric lights. No indoor plumbing, sanitation, or running water. Cleaning services were unavailable, and medical attention was scant. Forget about hot showers or clean linens. Forget about mercy. The stench was horrid; the food, filthy and insufficient. The men were always hungry. The primitive conditions were designed to strip prisoners of morale and hope. It was like being sealed alive in a slimy tomb without a ray of courage.

All of this had finally gotten to Prisoner B, and he was a broken man, overcome with suicidal despair. But a few yards away in the opposite cell, Prisoner A was more resolute. He was downright gutsy and seemed immune to giving up. Though he sometimes battled moments of discouragement—anyone would—he knew how to shake them off. He'd learned through many hard experiences how to make the best of any situation, even in the worst of circumstances. He was downright cheerful.

> Two men looked through prison bars.
> One saw mud; the other saw stars.

One day Prisoner B couldn't take it anymore. "What's wrong with you?" he shouted to his neighbor. "Don't you know we are doomed? We are lost? Don't you know we are going to starve to death, or freeze to death, or be beaten to death, or be tortured? Don't you realize no one cares any longer?"

Prisoner A looked up from the letter he was scribbling and clutched his thin blanket, tightening it across his shoulders.

"Are you talking to me?"

"Yeah, you. I am talking to you. I'm fed up with your cheerfulness. I am hurting. I am so miserable I want to die before this day ends, and any normal man in our circumstances would feel the same way. I think you're delusional."

There was a pause.

"Well, maybe I am," said the first prisoner at last. "But I've got some friends on the outside, and they've just sent me some money. I know how to get things. I can get us some food and some blankets and some underwear and some soap, and I'll share it with you. What I'm doing just now is writing a letter to thank them. At least, it started out as a thank you note; but I've gotten carried away. Looks like I've written a veritable epistle. Here, let me read a little of it to you . . . to get your opinion . . . just a few sentences. Would you listen?"

The second prisoner fell silent, so the first man continued.

"Here's what I wrote in the first part of the letter."

Now I want you to know, brothers and sisters, that what has happened to me has actually served to advance the gospel. As a result, it has become clear throughout the whole palace guard and to everyone else that I am in chains for Christ. And because of my chains, most of the brothers and sisters have become confident in the Lord and dare all the more to proclaim the gospel without fear. . . . I eagerly expect and hope that I will in no way be ashamed, but will have sufficient courage so that now as always Christ will be exalted in my body, whether by life or by death. For to me, to live is Christ and to die is gain. (Phil. 1:12–14, 20–21)

Pausing, Prisoner A looked at his jail mate and said, "I especially like that last sentence, don't you? It sums everything up very nicely. Here, let me read from the second part of the letter."

Prisoner B closed his eyes and slowly shook his head, not believing he was getting a sort of lecture. Undeterred, the first man continued reading.

In your relationships with one another, have the same mindset as Christ Jesus: Who, being in very nature God, did not consider equality with God something to be used to his own advantage; rather, he made himself nothing by taking the very nature of a servant, being made in human likeness. And being found in appearance as a man, he humbled himself by becoming obedient to death—even death on a cross! Therefore God exalted him to the highest place and gave him the name that is above every name, that at the name of Jesus every knee should bow, in heaven and on earth and under the earth, and every tongue acknowledge that Jesus Christ is Lord, to the glory of God the Father. (Phil. 2:5–11)

Pausing again, the first prisoner quipped, "I like the way that sounds, if I say so myself. It's downright inspired. Here's something from the third part of the letter."

One thing I do: Forgetting what is behind and straining toward what is ahead, I press on toward the goal to win the prize for which God has called me heavenward in Christ Jesus. All of us, then, who are mature should take such a view of things. (Phil. 3:13–15)

Prisoner B was listening at least, so Prisoner A told him with an understanding smile, "So my dear friend, while you sit there bemoaning the past and cursing the present, I'm planning the future. My best days are ahead of me, and I'm pressing forward with all my strength."

The second prisoner grunted.

The penman continued, "Now, when you interrupted me a few minutes ago I was just finishing the last part of my letter. Here, let me read it to you so you can tell me what you think."

Rejoice in the Lord always. I will say it again: Rejoice! Let your gentleness be evident to all. The Lord is near. Do not be anxious about anything, but in every situation by prayer and petition, with thanksgiving, present your requests to God. And the peace of God, which transcends all understanding, will guard your hearts and your minds in Christ Jesus. (Phil. 4:4–7)

The reader set his parchment on the stone slab and looked at his cellmate through the flickering shadows of the torchlight. "Anyway, if I seem in reasonable spirits, that's why. I've been working on this letter all week, and it's been therapeutic to me. I feel like I've been preaching to myself. The more I think about these things and write them down for others, the more I realize it is possible for me to stay in the best of spirits during the worst of times. I can do that. In fact, I can do all this through Jesus Christ who infuses me with strength."

Prisoner B absorbed this in silence. Then, running a filthy hand over his matted beard, he squinted across the dim corridor and said, "Then you must be saint Paul the apostle."

"Yes, well, that's what they call me. Now let me read you the conclusion of my note to my friends in Philippi. I'd like your reaction to it. They sent me a gift by the hand of Epaphroditus, and I'm sending him back with this letter. So here are my concluding thoughts."

I rejoiced greatly in the Lord that at last you renewed your concern for me. Indeed, you were concerned, but you had no opportunity to show it. I am not saying this because I am in need, for I have learned to be content whatever the circumstances. I know what it is to be in need, and I know what it is to have plenty. I have learned the secret of being content in any and every situation, whether well fed or hungry, whether living in plenty or in want. I can do all this through him who gives me strength.

Yet it was good of you to share in my troubles. Moreover, as you Philippians know, in the early days of your acquaintance with the gospel, when I set out from Macedonia, not one church shared with me in the matter of giving and receiving, except you only; for even when I was in Thessalonica, you sent me aid more than once when I was in need. Not that I desire your gifts; what I desire is that more be credited to your account. I have received full payment and have more than enough. I am amply supplied, now that I have received from Epaphroditus the gifts you sent. They are a fragrant offering, an acceptable sacrifice, pleasing to God.

And my God will meet all your needs according to the riches of his glory in Christ Jesus. (Phil. 4:10–19)

Whether Paul read his letter to a fellow prisoner is unknown, but it's clear he wrote Philippians from prison, probably in Rome, in response to the gift the Philippians had sent him via Epaphroditus. Prisoners in those days could send out and buy things if they had money, and this gift came when Paul most needed it. So he wrote them a thank you note, and he used it as an occasion to share his testimony and teaching throughout the entire book.

Near the end, he took the opportunity to express his appreciation to them. Even something as pedestrian as this, however, became an occasion for teaching for Paul. In verses 13 and 19, we have two tremendous verses: we can do all things through Christ, and Christ will meet all our needs according to the riches of His glory in Christ Jesus.

ALL . . . LEARNED . . . CONTENT

We can grasp the meaning of Philippians 4:13 by noticing three critical terms.

The first term is ALL. Notice it shows up in both verses 13 and 19: "I can do *all* this through him who gives me strength (NKJV) . . . and my God will meet *all* your needs according to the riches of his glory in Christ."

I've loved the word *all* in the Bible since discovering it in 1 Peter 5:7: "Cast *all* your anxiety on him because he cares for you." The word *all* is often grammatically unnecessary, and we would love these verses even if *all* wasn't there. But the word *all* magnifies the impact of the verses and extends their implications to infinity. Nothing is too small for God's care or too large for His keeping.

I once looked up every occurrence of the word *all* in Scripture and wrote a devotional book titled *All to Jesus.* Some of the Bible's greatest truths, promises, and commands are amplified by *all.*

- *In **all** things God works for the good of those who love him*—Romans 8:28
- *You have put **all** my sins behind your back*—Isaiah 38:17
- *Even the very hairs of your head are **all** numbered*—Matthew 10:30
- *Come to me, **all** you who are weary and burdened*—Matthew 11:28
- *Goodness and love will follow me **all** the days of my life*—Psalm 23:6
- *Seek first his kingdom and his righteousness, and **all** these things will be given to you*—Matthew 6:33

The word *all* isn't always used in the Bible in an absolute sense. Its specific meaning is always determined by its context. Sometimes the meaning of *all* is qualified by the passage. For example, here in Philippians 4:13, Paul said he could do all things through Christ who strengthened him. That's the way most translations render it. But Paul didn't mean to say he could literally do everything without qualification. I don't think he intended to say:

- I can do all things, so I'm going to be like Moses and raise my rod and send catastrophic plagues on the Roman empire.
- I can do all things, so I'm going to imitate Samson and tear this prison down with my bare hands.
- I can do all things, so I'll call fire down from heaven like Elijah.
- I can do all things, so I'm going to be like Jesus, levitate into the sky, and disappear into the clouds.

The apostle said "I can do all things," but he didn't mean he could do *those* things, for those things didn't represent God's will for his life. That's why the New International Version translated the verse with a nod to its context.

I have learned the secret of being content in any and every situation, whether well fed or hungry, whether living in plenty or in want. *I can do all this* through him who gives me strength. (Phil. 4:12–13)

Against the background of this passage, Paul was telling the Philippians: Jesus Christ is infusing me with strength in my inner being, allowing me to rejoice wherever He puts me and make the best of things in the worst of times. He is strengthening my perspective about contentment. He is enabling me to maintain a healthy attitude even while incarcerated by Rome.

The second word is *learned*. It occurs twice here, for Paul repeated himself for emphasis:

I have learned to be content whatever the circumstances. I know what it is to be in need, and I know what it is to have plenty. *I have learned* the secret of being content in any and every situation, whether well fed or hungry, whether living in plenty or in want. I can do all this through him who gives me strength. (Phil. 4:11–13)

This attitude of contentment was no more intuitive for Paul than for us. He wasn't naturally accepting of difficult situations. It wasn't instinctive for him to trust the Lord with limitations. This was an acquired education. It took time, spiritual maturing, emotional growth, and divine tutoring to get to this mind-set and perspective.

Just as we learn to ride a bicycle, perform specialized skills at work, or cook risotto, so we have to learn to function on a spiritual level, tackling life with the strength God makes available to us and being content whatever the circumstances.

The third word is *content*, which also appears twice.

I have learned to be *content* whatever the circumstances. I know what it is to be in need, and I know what it is to have plenty. I have learned the secret of being *content* in any and every situation, whether well fed or hungry, whether living in plenty or in want. I can do all this through him who gives me strength. (Phil. 4:11–13)

The word *content* is an insufficient translation of the Greek word here, but I can't find a better one. Paul didn't mean he was satisfied. He didn't mean he was complacent. He meant he was self-sufficient in his attitude. He meant his joy and cheer and purpose and resolution in life were not damaged by his circumstances. Whether he lived in a palace or a prison, he intended to have the same joy and sense of purpose. He could keep the best of spirits in the worst of conditions, for his perspective was strengthened by God's will and wisdom.

We haven't the ability to maintain positive attitudes through inborn dispositions or natural personalities. It's not a matter of possibility thinking or optimistic slogans. This kind of self-sufficiency is derived from a unique maturity fostered by the Lord who imparts supernatural strength.

That's the immediate interpretation of this verse. Paul was saying, "Whatever the circumstances, in any and every situation, I can be self-sufficient, I can be resilient, I can be unbreakable and undefeated and victorious in my attitude. I can make the most of things under the harshest of conditions through Him who enables me to do that. He infuses me with strength for this very thing. He strengthens my ability to remain resolute and positive, whatever happens."

Sometimes we're able to live without illness, travel where we want, pay our bills easily, avoid conflicts with our neighbors, and enjoy freedom from crippling problems. Other times we're in all kinds of distress or duress. But Paul learned to maintain a consistently strong spirit whatever the circumstances. Three times in Philippians 4, he used the words *situation* and *circumstance*.

- In verse 6, he said, "In every *situation*, by prayer and petition, with thanksgiving, present your requests to God."
- He declared in verse 11, "I have learned to be content whatever the *circumstances*."
- In verse 12 he spoke of being content "in any and every *situation*."

On this basis we can give God our whatevers and wherevers: *Whatever* represents His will for me, *whatever* He sends me and *wherever* He sends me, *whatever* He calls me to do—if it is His will and His way—He will strengthen me for it. *Whatever* attitudes He prescribes in the Bible, I can experience them. *Whatever* tasks He assigns, I can do them. *Whatever, whenever, wherever, however, whoever* . . . He will strengthen the infrastructure of my soul.

That means Philippians 4:13 has application to our lives every day in a multitude of circumstances. It's a verse we can claim in many different settings.

Recently I perused a book of devotions written by high school students for high school students. One of the entries was by Allison Fisher of Raleigh, North Carolina. "There are a lot of things teens can worry about in high school, which can make trusting God difficult," she said. "I worry about my grades, getting sick, disappointing my family, and whether people like me or not. When I worry, I like to pray. Every time I have to take a test, I sit at my desk and pray before I start. Some people look at me funny, but it is just something I do. It always helps me feel better. When I am nervous about a big test or going through something difficult, one of my favorite verses to think of is Philippians 4:13, which says, 'I am able to do all things through Him who strengthens me.'"[1]

I read something similar by pastor and author Dr. Charles Stanley. He said Philippians 4:13 was a great help to him when he was a young person. He knew there were certain things he needed in his life, such as guidance and encouragement. On one occasion, he said, he was concerned about his grades in school. But he leaned on verses he found in the Bible. "One of my favorites is Philippians 4:13, 'I can do all things through Him who strengthens me,'" said Stanley. "I realized with His help I could do whatever He had given me to do."[2]

Years ago when I was a young fellow working in the Billy Graham crusades, I remember hearing Dr. Graham confess that sometimes before speaking to a vast crowd in a stadium, he would grow fearful, unsure if he could do it. But before leaving the dressing room, he said, he would close his eyes and meditate on Philippians 4:13.[3]

Another minister, Ed Underwood, came to Christ during the Jesus Movement of the 1960s and 1970s. He's now pastor of the Church of the Open Door in Southern California. In his book *When God Breaks*

Your Heart, he wrote openly of his battle with malevolent lymphoma, a form of cancer oncologists claim leads to more suicides than any other form. It can produce intense pain and unbearable itching, which, according to Underwood, can push the senses and the psyche to the limit.

"My unique pain centers on the flaming, all-consuming irritation of my skin," Underwood wrote. "The agony was excruciating. First the heat, then the insane itching, finally the weakness as my body began shaking from the effect of exfoliating skin."

He described his pain so vividly I almost felt it as I read his account of blood boring upward to the surface of the skin and heating it until it exfoliated, causing searing itching and intense pain.

Ed wrote, "Falling back on some of my favorite verses from the Scripture, or the most comforting truths about the personal relationship with the Lord Jesus I entered into as a young man, I repeat the verse or truth over and over again. I always begin with Philippians 4:13, a sentence from my Father's Word that has seen me through these despairing times: 'I can do all things through Christ who strengthens me.' Then I discipline my mind to say this over again and again with the emphasis on a different word each time."

> **I** can do all things through Christ who strengthens me.
> I **can** do all things through Christ who strengthens me.
> I can **do** all things through Christ who strengthens me.
> I can do **all** things through Christ who strengthens me.
> I can do all **things** through Christ who strengthens me.
> I can do all things **through** Christ who strengthens me.
> I can do all things through **Christ** who strengthens me.
> I can do all things through Christ **who strengthens** me.
> I can do all things through Christ who strengthens **me**.[4]

"This is not a 'technique' to pull out of your spiritual hat in a moment of need," he wrote. "This is a therapy for those who walk with Him. It is only by abiding in His love and guidance as we walk by the still waters of everyday life and learn to trust Him for the minor emergencies and disappointments that we gain the strength of faith and comforting truths that will steel our soul in our personal day of trouble."[5]

Rejoice wherever God puts you. Rejoice in the Lord always. When you look through bars, see stars. Don't worry about the power of positive thinking; just dwell on the positive power of an eternal God. And remember Georg Neumark's old hymn:

> *If thou but suffer God to guide thee*
> *And hope for Him through all thy ways,*
> *He'll give thee strength, whate'er betide thee,*
> *And bear thee through the evil days.*

A WORD FROM KATRINA

Robert and I had a bug; I'm not even sure what it was. We never got critically sick, but we were both under the weather and both very weak. In fact, our primary symptom was extreme weakness. Rob was committed to helping me, especially with our evening routines. At that time I was doing more for myself, but the illness exacerbated my helplessness.

He could hardly stand on his feet, yet he had to lift and carry and position and help me. I wasn't sure he could even bend over to put his arms beneath me, but as he did so I heard him whispering something. "What are you saying?" I asked.

He said, "I can do all things through Christ who strengthens me." Boy, did that encourage me! I figured if he could pray that so he could be strong to help me, I could and would do the same thing.

I have never forgotten that and have uttered that prayer many times. It is true—with Christ we can certainly conquer, with faith, all the trials, inconveniences, sicknesses, and tests our lives throw at us. Jesus is overflowing with power and strength for our journey here below.

Power Lines

L ast night I stood on the front porch and watched the sun descend like a burning plate behind the horizon. This morning while brushing my teeth, I saw the same sun arise on the opposite side, ascending over the tree line like a blazing disk. I thought of the old song "Awake, my soul, and with the sun thy daily stage of duty run."[1]

Who knows how many days are left us in this world? How long until the Lord returns? Not long, I think. We have work to do and a cause to advance, and we need all the strength we can muster.

We almost titled this book *From Strength to Strength*, based on a phrase in Psalm 84. There the writer described his anticipation for an upcoming trip. He was packing his bags for Jerusalem, preparing for his regular pilgrimage to Mount Zion for one of the periodic festivals of Israel.

"My soul yearns, even faints, for the courts of the LORD," he said in verse 2.

But the trip was rigorous, dangerous, and demanding. Where would he find strength for the journey? He especially dreaded the hot valley of Baka, nicknamed the Arid Valley or the Valley of Weeping. But he was undaunted. He was eager for the trip, believing it would be blessed. He exclaimed:

Blessed are those whose strength is in you,
whose hearts are set on pilgrimage.
As they pass through the Valley of Baka,
they make it a place of springs;
the autumn rains also cover it with pools.
They go from strength to strength,
till each appears before God in Zion. (Ps. 84:5–7)

Our lives are a pilgrimage, which is an encouraging perspective. Who wants to settle down here? I'm looking forward to the city whose architect and builder is God. But until then, we're travelers hiking through rugged terrain. As we press on, strengthened by the Lord, we'll leave blessings behind us. We'll turn waterless valleys into irrigated landscapes.

That's the influence we wield as we travel toward heaven and toward home. We go from strength to strength, from day to day, from faith to faith, and from glory to glory.

Along the way, the Lord will provide all the strength we need. Those who set their hearts on pilgrimage go from strength to strength till we all appear before God in Zion.

Just remember these simple lines from Scripture—God's power lines stretching from heaven to energize your life wherever you are in the journey:

- As your days may demand shall your strength always be.
- The eyes of the Lord range to and fro throughout all the earth to strengthen those whose hearts are fully committed to Him.
- The joy of the Lord is your strength.
- The Lord is our refuge and strength.
- In quietness and trust is your strength.
- Those who wait on the Lord will renew their strength.
- The Lord will strengthen your frame.

- The sovereign Lord is your strength; He makes your feet like the feet of a deer and enables you to tread on the heights.
- Love the Lord your God with all your strength.
- Be strengthened in faith, fully persuaded God has the power to do what He has promised.
- Do all this through Him who strengthens you.
- Out of His glorious riches He will strengthen you with power through His Spirit in your inner being. Now to Him who is able to do immeasurably more than all we ask or imagine according to His power at work within us, to Him be glory.

I want to devote my last drops of ink to thanking my publisher, Matt Baugher, whose encouragement is infectious; my editor, Adria Haley; the marketing team, led by Lori Cloud; and my literary agents, Sealy Yates and Matt Yates, whose advice is invaluable. I owe a huge debt of gratitude to Joshua Rowe and his colleagues at Clearly Media. And undying appreciation goes to the staff and attenders at The Donelson Fellowship in Nashville. My assistant, Sherry Anderson, is a lifesaver; and I appreciate Casey Pontious, who labored through her pregnancy, so to speak, securing annotations and permissions.

Our three daughters—Victoria, Hannah, and Grace—and their husbands and children are a continual source of strength.

And most of all . . . Katrina, who inadvertently birthed this book while asking for a couple of extra strength pills.

Like any sensible husband, I'll give her the last word.

A FINAL WORD FROM KATRINA

Blessed are those whose strength is in you, whose hearts are set on pilgrimage. . . . They go from strength to strength, till each appears before God in Zion. (Ps. 84:5, 7)

"Life is a journey" sounds like a cliché, but it's an image drawn from the Bible. As I look back at my life, I identify with the idea of pilgrimage.

I grew up in a Finnish home in a Finnish community in West Paris, Maine, and I attended a Finnish-speaking church with my mother. When I was nine, a Sunday school campaign stressed Scripture memory, and I won a free week at Camp Clear in Cape Cod, Massachusetts. While there one night at a campfire meeting, the speaker presented the gospel. He said Jesus died on the cross for our sins and rose again on the third day. That's when I gave my life to the Lord, though I didn't say anything about it at the time.

Shortly afterward, we began attending West Paris Baptist Church, which was English-speaking, and that's where I went forward for baptism. Soon afterward I was baptized in a nearby pond. Paul and Heather Danielson were pastoring then, who were alumni of Columbia International University in South Carolina.

After high school, I attended secretarial school in Portland, Maine, and was hired by a wealthy lady in Palm Beach, Florida, as her assistant. Mrs. Johnson, a zealous Christian, became my mentor.

In 1973, the doors opened for me to attend Columbia International University because of a secretarial position on the staff there. That's where I met Robert, who was a graduating senior. He was a speaker for a team representing the school, and I was hired as the assistant for that department. He and I worked together almost every day on itineraries and details of team trips.

One weekend his team needed a staff chaperone, so they asked me. When I heard Rob speak, I fell head over heels in love with him. He moved on to Wheaton, but in 1976 we were married. After a year living in Roan Mountain, Tennessee, we began pastoring in nearby Greeneville on our first wedding anniversary.

Since then God has given us three daughters, more than a dozen grandkids, nearly four decades in ministry, and a prolonged struggle with disability. As I write this, I've been on my own while my husband is overseas, but I've been thinking of how my whole life is a personification of the verses in Psalm 84 about going from strength to strength.

My handicap brings me the same obstacles every day, and it has been encouraging to experience the same breakthroughs each day—literally from strength to strength. It's not automatic; the maneuvering of legs and the deliberate pressure on my feet is gained by acts of faith resulting in strength yesterday and then again today.

This is very encouraging. He helped me before, so I know He will do it again. Each time I act in faith, He gives me strength to do the simple but difficult activities that comprise my days. God is committed to strengthening that which concerns me.

You and I both need extra strength for those extra tasks that fill our hours. Let's pray for each other, solidify our determination to follow Christ, and press toward the goal of a productive life that fulfills God's plan for each day.

Notes

Introduction

1. The hymn "O God, of All the Strength and Power" is attributed to Ambrose of Milan (c. 340–397), and the words of the 1875 English translation are credited to John M. Neale.

2. This phrase occurs in the hymn "Great Is Thy Faithfulness" by Thomas Chisholm, 1923.

Chapter 1: Connect to a High Voltage Line

1. William Osborn Stoddard, *Grover Cleveland* (New York: Frederick A. Stocks & Brother, 1888), 213. Also see Harriet Putnam, *Lives of the Presidents in Words of One Syllable* (New York: McLoughlin Brothers, 1903), 121.

2. This hymn was published in 1787 in *A Selection of Hymns from the Best Authors,* compiled by John Rippon. The identity of the author cannot be confirmed, but some hymnologists believe it was written by John Keene.

3. See, for example, the article "The Economic Miracle of Israel's Natural Gas Fields" by Tsvi Sadan in *Israel Today,* September 29, 2014, at www.israeltoday.co.il/Default.aspx?tabid=178&nid=25370. Or the article, "Israel's Big Gusher" by Martin Fletcher, in *Slate* magazine, February 26, 2014, at www.slate.com/articles/news_and_politics/moment/2014/02/israel_s_natural_gas_deposits_tel_aviv_s_offshore_gas_fields_will_make_it.html.

4. Verses 26–29, which conclude Moses' blessings on the tribes of Israel, were probably addressed to the whole nation. The specific blessing to Asher seems

to be contained in Deuteronomy 33:24–25. With verse 26, Moses concluded by blessing the totality of the tribes, of which Asher, of course, was one. In that sense, the entire passage, verses 24–29, was applicable to Asher.

5. English Standard Version.

6. Robert J. Morgan, *Mastering Life Before It's Too Late* (Nashville: Howard Publications, 2015), 193.

7. Adapted from Michael Richardson, *Amazing Faith: The Authorized Biography of Bill Bright* (Colorado Springs: WaterBrook Press, 2000), 12–24.

8. *The Living Bible.*

9. From Charles Haddon Spurgeon's sermon, "As Thy Days, So Shall Thy Strength Be," August 22, 1858, at www.spurgeon.org/sermons/0210.htm.

10. Lucy G. Thurston, *Life and Times of Mrs. Lucy G. Thurston, wife of Rev. Asa Thurston, Pioneer Mission to the Sandwich Islands* (Ann Arbor, MI, 1882), 168–175.

11. Elisabeth Elliot, *Secure in the Everlasting Arms* (Ann Arbor, MI: Servant Publications, 2002).

12. Patricia Knight, *Pure Joy* (Fairfax, VA: Xulon Press, 2003), 248.

Chapter 2: Turn Messes into Momentum

1. There's been recent criticism of the genre of missionary biography and autobiography as sanitized, romanticized, and unrealistic. But everyone has a story to tell, and no biography is complete or unbiased. While biographical literature should be realistic, no biography shows every wart, flaw, or depressing episode. The same criticism could be leveled against political biographies, sports biographies, and the stories of pastors and Christian business leaders. I encourage everyone—especially missionaries—to record their stories in a way that reflects their own experiences, and I hope we'll see a renaissance of missionary biography.

2. Mabel Francis, *One Shall Chase a Thousand* (Harrisburg, PA: Christian Publications, Inc., 1968), 83.

3. www.send.org.

4. Mabel Francis, *One Shall Chase a Thousand* (Harrisburg, PA: Christian Publications, Inc., 1968), 103–104.

5. From the hymn "O, for a Faith that Will Not Shrink" by William H. Bathurst, in *Psalms and Hymns,* published in 1831.

6. "Come, Thou Fount of Every Blessing" by Robert Robinson, written in 1757 when the hymnist was 22 years old.

7. Francis Schaeffer, *He Is There and He Is Not Silent* (Carol Stream, IL: Tyndale House Publishers, 1972).

8. Mason Currey, introduction to *Daily Rituals: How Artists Work* (New York: Alfred A. Knopf, 2013).

9. For more about establishing a daily plan for Bible study and prayer, see my book *Mastering Life Before It's Too Late*.

Chapter 3: Invest in a Power Company

1. *A History of Cleveland and Its Environs, Vol III: Biography* (Chicago, IL: The Lewis Publishing Company, 1918), 258–259.

2. Ibid. Also see *Quarterly Review of the Alumni Association of the University of Michigan*, Volume LV, Number 20, May 7, 1949, in an article by Fred C. Kelly about Charles F. Brush, 244.

3. The Charles F. Brush, Sr. Papers, library.case.edu/ksl/collections/special /manuscripts/brush/brushfinding.html. Also, *The Literary Digest: Vol IX, No. 16*, August 18, 1894, 15.

4. In the article "Charles F. Brush" by Fred C. Kelly in the *Michigan Alumnus Quarterly Review*, Volume 55, Number 20, May 7, 1949, 243.

5. *The Voice.*

6. *Christian History & Biography* magazine, Issue 82, Spring 2004, 13.

7. This poem was reportedly printed on a postcard at Ocean Park, New York, in the Casterline Card series, number 5510 (undated). Casterline was a postcard company started by Helen A. Casterline of Buffalo, New York.

8. King James Version.

Chapter 4: Occupy a Fortress

1. New King James Version.

2. The reference to the caged bird is from the Taylor Prism in the British Museum.

3. From the hymn "Rock of Ages" by Augustus M. Toplady, published in 1776.

4. "Under His Wings" by William O. Cushing, published in 1896.

5. "When You Sing Next Sunday, Thank Luther" by Richard D. Dinwiddie, in *Christianity Today*, October 21, 1983, 19.

6. David Jeremiah, *A Bend in the Road* (Nashville: Thomas Nelson, 2000), chapter 10.

7. New King James Version.

8. Jonathan Edwards, *The Works of Jonathan Edwards, Vol. II* (London: Ball, Arnold, and Co., 1840), 932.

9. *The Voice.*

10. New King James Version.

11. *Hymns for Divine Worship* (London: William Cooke, 1868), Number 131, 96.

12. Based on personal conversations and email. Used with permission.

13. Psalm 46 ("God Is Our Refuge and Our Strength") from the 1650 Scottish Psalter. You can find the entire hymn online at www.hymntime.com/tch/htm /g/i/s/gisourrs.htm.

Chapter 5: Stand Sequoia-Like Above the Noise

1. King James Version.

2. Personal interview and correspondence with Elena Chevalier. Used with permission.

3. Anne Cram, "The Hidden Word," in the devotional book *Morning Praise: 365 Devotions for Women by Women,* edited by Ardis Dick Stenbakken (Hagerstown, MD: Review and Herald Publishing Association, 2006), 296.

4. "In Quietness and Confidence" by Rev. George Wilson of Edinburgh, in *Good Words for 1888,* edited by Donald Macleod (London: Isbister and Company, 1888), 770.

5. King James Version.

6. Personal conversation with Sam Doherty. Used with permission.

7. http://www.theconstructionindex.co.uk/news/view/noise-cancelling-fences -in-development.

8. Bernard Gilpin, *Memorials of the Life and Ministry of Bernard Gilpin* (London: J. C. Pembray, 1874), 319.

9. Annie Jenkins Sallee, *W. Eugene Sallee: God's Ambassador* (Nashville: The Sunday School Board of the Southern Baptist Convention, 1933), 42.

Chapter 6: Catch Updrafts Like an Eagle

1. www.altenergy.org/renewables/solar.html.

2. I'm indebted to my late professor at Columbia International University, James Hatch, who taught brilliantly and poignantly on the prophets, and especially on Isaiah. Some of the material in this chapter is taken from my memories of his lectures forty years ago.

3. The quotes from John R. Rice are from his book *God's Cure for Anxious*

Care (Murfreesboro, TN: Sword of the Lord Publishers, 1948), chapter 4, "Power to the Faint."

4. My notes from a private conversation with Ruth Bell Graham in 1971.

5. Personal interview and correspondence. Used with permission.

Chapter 7: Strengthen Someone Else

1. In the foreword of *How Christianity Changed the World* by Alvin J. Schmidt (Grand Rapids: Zondervan, 2004), 8–9.

2. Widely reported by all major news outlets, including NBC News at www
.nbcnews.com/storyline/ebola-virus-outbreak/ebola-survivor-dr-kent-brantlys
-full-remarks-god-saved-my-n185956.

3. www.unicef.org/media/media_68359.html.

4. Based on recollection.

5. For more information, visit www.zimorphancare.org or e-mail Alan Graham at alang@zimorphancare.org.

6. Based on a personal conversation with Alan Graham. Used with permission.

Chapter 8: Process Your Problems and Arrive at Praise

1. Steven James, *Story Trumps Structure* (Cincinnati: Writer's Digest Books, 2014), 6–7.

2. This reference is used with permission.

3. Rabbi Simlai had a few other references that he felt contained Hebrew summaries of the Law. You can find his analysis in the entry on Simlai in *Cyclopaedia of Biblical, Theological, and Ecclesiastical Literature, Volume 9,* edited by John McClintock (New York: Harper & Brothers, 1889), 752.

4. Romans 1:17; Galatians 3:11; and Hebrews 10:38.

5. *The Message.*

6. Gregg Matte, *Finding God's Will* (Grand Rapids: Baker Books, 2010), quotes from chapter 7: "The Part of God's Will No One Wants."

7. Words and music by Don Francisco.

Chapter 9: Strike a Missing Chord

1. "Paulo Coelho Explains Why Courage Is the Most Important Spiritual Quality," September 9, 2014, at www.huffingtonpost.com/2014/09/09/paulo

-coelho-alchemist-spiritual-people_n_5786482.html?utm_hp_ref=own&ir
=OWN.

2. Quoted by John Grasso, Bill Mallon, and Jeroen Heijmans in *Historical Dictionary of the Olympic Movement* (Lanham, MD: Rowman & Littlefield, 2015), 421.

3. http://www.brainyquote.com/quotes/quotes/a/audreyhepb413489.html?src =t_the_most_important.

4. "Taylor Swift Confesses She Doesn't Fit In," at http://hollywoodlife.com /2014/08/27/taylor-swift-video-outtakes-shake-it-off/.

5. Helen Roseveare, *Living Sacrifice: Willing to Be Whittled as an Arrow.*

6. Fr. M. K. Paul, *Best Wishes for Your Retired Life* (The Bombay Saint Paul Society, 2007), 23. Most of the versions of this story identify Printz as Sweden's Consul to Canada, but an Internet search of old newspapers demonstrated he was a native Norwegian who served as the Norwegian Consul General in Toronto. See, for example, *The Evening Citizen,* Ottawa, Ontario, Thursday, December 4, 1941, page 5.

7. Nesta de Robeck, *The Life of St. Francis of Assisi* (Assisi, Italy: Casa Editrice Franciscana, 2000), 42.

Chapter 10: Galvanize Yourself Against Discouragement

1. Personal story told to me and communicated with an e-mail. At her request, I've changed the name. Used with permission.

2. *Forbidden Harvest,* pp. 41–42.

3. My quoting of this psalm is my own version made up of bits and pieces of various translations, which I've memorized.

4. From Charles Haddon Spurgeon's sermon "Songs in the Night," February 27, 1898, at www.spurgeon.org/sermons/2558.php.

Chapter 11: Live Like the Rich Person You Are

1. http://www.slate.com/blogs/moneybox/2014/09/24/facts_about_ billionaires
_data_from_the_2014_wealth_x_and_ubs_billionaire.html.

2. Arthur T. Pierson, *The Gospel: Volume 1* (Grand Rapids: Baker, 1978), 160.

3. Wade C. Graber, *The Mission of the Holy Spirit* (New York: Innova Publishing, 2010), segment 33.

4. "A Child of the King" by Harriet E. Buell, 1877.

5. English Standard Version.

6. English Standard Version.
7. Adapted from Arthur T. Pierson, *The Gospel: Volume 1* (Grand Rapids: Baker, 1978), 161–163.
8. From the hymn "Lord, Speak to Me" by Frances Ridley Havergal, written in 1872.
9. Personal interview and email with Roy Harrison. Used by permission.

Chapter 12: Learn to Rejoice Whatever, Whenever, Wherever

1. Allison Fisher, *Teen to Teen: 365 Daily Devotions by Teen Girls for Teen Girls,* edited by Patti M. Hummel (Nashville: B&H Publishing Group, 2013), 119.
2. Charles Stanley, *10 Principles for Studying Your Bible* (Nashville: Thomas Nelson, 1008), 131.
3. My undocumented recollections from the 1970s.
4. Ed Underwood, *When God Breaks Your Heart: Choosing Hope in the Midst of Faith-Shattering Circumstances* (Colorado Springs: David C. Cook, 2008), 165–166.
5. Ibid., 170.

Conclusion: Power Lines

1. By Thomas Ken, written in 1664.

Also Available from Robert J. Morgan

NOW INCLUDES NEW STUDY QUESTIONS

THE SAME GOD WHO LED
YOU IN WILL LEAD YOU OUT

THE
RED SEA
RULES

10
GOD-GIVEN
STRATEGIES
for
DIFFICULT TIMES

ROBERT J. MORGAN

ISBN: 9780529104403

True Peace Starts Here.

Rob Morgan unlocks the peace of meditation in a biblically sound way. New Age meditation tells us to empty our minds, but biblical meditation tells us to fill our minds with the Lord. In *Reclaiming the Lost Art of Biblical Meditation*, Rob will show the biblical foundation of the practice, give insight into making it a part of your daily faith, and other practical applications to deepen your faith through meditation.

Available April 2017